FOR THE STRENGTH OF
HARLEM
PLĔAS TUSANT PEARSON

Janell Pearson

STRENGTH POINT PUBLISHING, INC.

Our books may be purchased in bulk for promotional, educational, or business use. Please contact your local bookseller or Strength Point Publishing, Inc. by email at: info@strengthpointpublishing.com

First published in the United States by
Strength Point Publishing, Inc.

First Edition
10 9 8 7 6 5 4 3 2 1

ISBN Paperback: 979-8-98696-32-1-1
ISBN Hardback: 979-8-98696-32-0-4
ISBN ebook: 979-8-98696-32-02-8
Audio file: 979-8-98696-32-3-5

Library of Congress Control Number: 2022918828
Names: Pearson, Janell, author.
Title: For the strength of Harlem – Plĕas Tusant Pearson / Janell Pearson.
Description: Includes bibliographical references. | East Stroudsburg, PA: Strength Point Publishing, Inc., 2022.
Identifiers: LCCN: 2022918828 | ISBN: 979-8-98696-32-0-4 (hardcover) | 979-8-98696-32-1-1 (paperback) | 979-8-98696-32-02-8 (ebook) | 979-8-98696-32-3-5 (audio)
Subjects: LCSH Pearson, Plĕas Tusant. | Harlem (New York, N.Y.)--Biography. | African Americans--New York (State)--New York--Biography. | Cooks--New York (State)--New York--Biography. | Harlem (New York, N.Y.)--History. | Harlem (New York, N.Y.)--Social conditions. | African Americans--New York (State)--New York--History. | BISAC BIOGRAPHY & AUTOBIOGRAPHY / Cultural, Ethnic & Regional / African American & Black | BIOGRAPHY & AUTOBIOGRAPHY / Historical | HISTORY / African American & Black | COOKING / Regional & Ethnic / Soul Food | COOKING / History
Classification: LCC F128.68.H3 .P43 P43 2022 | DDC 974.71/092--dc23

In memory of

Plĕas Tusant Pearson and Lucille Pearson,

you are truly missed!

Contents

Preface

A famous photograph exists of Malcolm X and Muhammad Ali walking through the streets of Harlem in the early '60s, basking in the admiration and adulation of their supporters. That photograph, taken by Howard Bingham, is instantly recognizable by many, and appears in the National Civil Rights Museum, as well as various African American museums, documentaries, publications, and websites. Among other historical books, the photo also appears in Muhammad Ali's memoir: *His Life and Times* by Thomas Hauser. Yet, viewers of this famous photograph often wonder, who is that man in the middle? Half visible behind the famous visages of those eminent figures striding before him; that slender, mustached face belongs to none other than my father, Plĕas Tusant Pearson (pronounced Plĕz).

While not as well-known beyond the borders of Harlem as the other two, Plĕas was, in his own right, a remarkable man, adored by his friends and family, and committed to uplifting his people to the next level. He belongs to a precious group of unsung heroes, tied to our past, existing in our present, who work diligently to affect positive change in our world. I believe it is crucially important for us to recognize the efforts of all the "men (and women) in the middle," whose lives affected so many. This book is one attempt to bring an unsung hero's tale to light, and I hope there will be many more to follow.

We acknowledge the popular and well-known Black leaders, we should also give tribute to all the unsung heroes, for they are not forgotten. Their stories simply have not been told yet!

When I think of my father, I remember his optimism, his unique perspectives, and his zest for life, learning, and adventure. His unflagging efforts to fight for racial justice that included founding a movement to end discrimination against Black construction workers in Harlem, and many other ventures helped members of the community. His efforts resulted in the sons of two prominent American Presidents—Franklin Delano Roosevelt Jr. and Vice President son— John Davison Rockefeller Jr. reaching out to Plĕas for his support.

At the same time, he was a renowned chef and owned a private limousine service that chauffeured celebrities to and from the Apollo at a time when yellow cabs refused to venture north of 125th Street. His wisdom, serial entrepreneurship, and commitment to the flourishing of Harlem and its residents inspired the title of this book. I hope others will be entertained and inspired by his life story. His family and community loved Plĕas, and I miss him terribly. This book is for him.

Malcolm X, Plĕas Tusant Pearson, and Muhammad Ali walking the streets of Harlem 1963.

"The man in the middle."
Photo taken by Howard L. Bingham

Introduction:
Memories And Memorabilia

Walking into my father's West Side Manhattan apartment after his death was like venturing into a vault of memories. Photographs of people he knew—famous actors, politicians, musicians, certificates he received and even gangsters from the Copacabana—crowded the walls in the hallway. Arranged on the shelves, facing his bed were gold-framed photographs of his family: his mother and father, brother, children and grandchildren. They were most important to him, and their faces were the first thing he saw every day when he woke up.

This was the apartment my father lived in since the early '70s, when his activism in the political movement he founded to advocate for Black construction workers made him a target for the white cops who patrolled Harlem's streets. His daunting words replay in a recurring loop in my mind. He said, "If I even spit on the ground, I'll be arrested and sent to jail for five years, with additional charges added on to make it stick."

He would further say: "You never know what you look like until you get your picture took." The apartment was a perfect picture of my dad. It captured his love for his family, his beloved memories of Harlem, and his penchant for knowledge about cooking, history, and travel.

When he moved into the seven-story brick building, it was populated with a multi-cultural mix of actors, musicians, writers, dancers, and regular working stiffs. I remember my father telling me about weekend parties in this building featuring performances by poets, actors, and musicians. Living here gave him an appreciation for diversity and an understanding of the education and perspective that came from learning about other cultures and languages.

Reflecting this fact were the many books about travel, cooking, and history, *Ebony* and *Jet* magazines, saved editions of The Amsterdam newspaper, and boxes of newspaper and magazine clippings on topics that interested him. His well-stocked and ordered kitchen carried the memories from decades of delicious meals based on recipes handed down to him by his mother and grandmother. Now, his white apron hung poignantly from a thumbtack next to the stove, like an eager puppy waiting for someone to toss the ball.

I comforted myself with the knowledge that I took the time, while he was alive, to record his voice with all his savvy, street-smart sayings and the great Harlem memories and insights he shared with me. Tragically, when I retrieved the box with the tape recorder and tapes from my closet after he died, I found that the battery had exploded, and the acid leaked all over the box. Thankfully, I took notes when he spoke, and of course, I have my memories. With these tools, I reconstructed the events of my father's life to the best of my ability and formed my father's story. I knew I could not let the destruction of those tapes silence his voice, and I hope you will hear it, as I still do, through the anecdotes in these pages. Plĕas was a truly powerful man, and to know him, was to love him.

From his turbulent roots in racially segregated Birmingham, Alabama, of the 1930s and '40s, to his adult life in Harlem, New York, Plĕas always fought for the rights of Black people and wanted to preserve the culture and dignity of Harlem as a Black community. He foresaw the gentrification of Harlem fifty years before he passed and started a movement to protect its culture and the potential displacement of Black businesses and habitation. Yet, Plĕas always maintained a gracious and upbeat spirit that attracted people to him from every tier of society—from needy families to famous athletes, politicians, and musicians. He treated everyone equally and expected the same.

As a father, Plĕas was equally encouraging and consistently made me feel positive and confident. I remember when he called me some years before he passed.

He could tell just by my voice what type of mood I was in. He used to find the funniest things to say to get me to laugh.

He said, "Right now, at this defining moment, you are still the most beautiful and the smartest girl in my life."

I laughed and said, "Daddy, I got rollers in my hair and Noxzema on my face!"

He said, "That's okay. You didn't look that way the other day or last week. You were fly then and now. Now, what's happening with you? Run it!"

Chapter 1

Growing up in Birmingham Under Jim Crow

Tusant Pearson Sr.,
18xx-19xx

Bessie Pearson,
1894-1951

Plĕas was born in Birmingham, Alabama, on December 12, 1922, to Bessie and Tusant Plĕas Pearson, Sr. Bessie admired Tusant Sr., and it was love at first sight; one thing she realized was that he would be her first and last love.

They courted for a short while, and then Tusant Sr. went to Bessie's mother to get her approval to marry Bessie. Emma knew of him but nothing really bad about his reputation. She knew he was a few years older than Bessie, but he seemed so sincere. In a way, he was a little too flashy, but he had big dreams.

Tusant Sr. revealed all the businesses he was going to open up, and she was somewhat impressed. She also thought that he would be a good provider for Bessie, so she agreed to allow Bessie to marry him.

They lived in a row house, with cedar floors and a pot-bellied stove in the colored section of town near Bessie's mother, Emma, who helped with the cooking and housework. After he bought it, Tusant fixed it up as best as possible, and Plĕas remembered a warm and loving household filled with the smells of fine food and the sounds of gospel music playing on the record player.

Plĕas' father was a traveling salesman, and Plĕas used to love to listen as he explained to Bessie how he sold his wares and figured out how to approach and engage potential clients. He often bought her beautiful dresses during his travels, but he encouraged her to be tough, too. He taught her how to shoot a rifle and a pistol in case she needed to protect the family while he was away—and she was a great shot!

In those days, Black men took whatever work ensured ends were met. So, when he wasn't selling, Tusant, Sr. put on a pair of boots and helped shovel coal for the railroad. He carried people's bags and did odd jobs—whatever was needed to feed his family. But he always taught Plĕas and his brother Johnnie that the most important thing for a Black man was to believe in himself because he couldn't afford to think any other way. He also taught them to think creatively about how to manage money. There was always a way; you just had to set your mind to it.

Of all his father's teachings, the ones Plĕas remembered most and adopted for himself were: Always respect females; aspire to be your best self

and represent yourself with pride and dignity. Above all else, never let any white man tell you that you are less than a man. Following his insights, Tusant asked his boys if they understood. Their answer was always the same. A resounding, "Yes, Sir!"

At 5'9", Bessie was a tall, dark-complexioned woman who loved to wear long, pearl necklaces and dressed with style. When she did not wear her hair pinned up, it hung naturally in long, flowing waves to her shoulders. A straight shooter, she was active in the community and ensured those around her had what they needed. People helped each other more back then, so when she heard someone didn't have food, wood, or coal to heat their house, she'd tell them to *come on over*. Black people knew "it took a village." No matter how tough things got, they were always there to support one another. Bessie was also an ambitious woman, and her aspirations to do something meaningful with her life ultimately came true when circumstances compelled her to start her own business.

Tusant, Sr. was a proud, respectable man, slim with strong features and a dapper dresser. He knew appearances counted, and even though he only owned two suits, he knew how to turn those two into four by mixing and matching the pants and the jackets, then topped the ensemble off with a tie, a flat-top hat, and a pair of two-tone shoes. Later in life, Plĕas took his father's attention to appearances to heart and said, "When you're walking in the street, you must know how you'll appear to people; how you'll be perceived."

Growing up under the devastating, racially segregating laws of Jim Crow, Plĕas, his brother Johnnie and their parents lived in a close-knit, Black neighborhood. People struggled to make it, but they supported one another and always found a way to lift each other's spirits. Food and music were a big part of that. Even in rough times, music always brought joy to people's hearts. They made instruments from pots and pans, strings, and washboards, and of course, they knew that nobody could take your voice, and no one could take your soul. So, soul food and soul music were available to everyone. You could buy entry into a juke joint for a nickel—a decorated shack that throbbed with great music and joyful spirits.

Whenever they ventured into the white part of town, Black people encountered a world clearly demarcated with signs for "Whites" and "Colored." That included everything from libraries to parks and drinking fountains, and most especially for Plĕas and his brother, school.

A.H. Parker High School was the only high school for colored students, and by the mid-1940s, the school was so crowded that classes had to be held day and night, with graduation ceremonies in January and June. Nevertheless, graduating was a badge of honor and a golden ticket to a better future. Around the dinner table, proud parents who hadn't had the opportunity to get an education themselves listened avidly to what their children learned in school.

The school had a rigorous academic program, offering nursing and printing mechanics classes, as well as traditional academics. Students took the dress code seriously, so girls wore dresses or skirts and blouses, while boys wore white shirts with a tie and belted black or blue trousers. Teaching was considered a prestigious career, so the teachers were revered and respected. The students understood that their teachers were helping them prepare for a better life.

Years later, in 1963—the same year Howard Bingham took the famous picture of Plĕas with Malcom X and Muhammad Ali—many students from Parker rallied with Dr. Martin Luther King's peaceful crusade to end segregation. Police subsequently ambushed them with attack dogs and water cannons. These students were members of King's "Foot Soldiers for Freedom" and, decades after Plĕas and his peers actively advocated for civil rights in Birmingham, they still fought. The youths organized protests and communicated via walkie-talkies, regarding where and when a protest was to take place. On May 3rd, 1963, after around six hundred children were arrested at a peaceful March, they gathered en masse at the 16th Street Baptist Church and heard Dr. King speak. He said, "If they think today is the end of this, they will be badly mistaken." Tragically, a few months later, this same church was bombed by the Ku Klux Klan on September 15th, killing four young girls.

Adding to the injustice of Jim Crow, white students often hung around outside the high school, with the intention of provoking a fight with anyone that clutched their books a little too tightly to their chests; their determined eyes focused on a better future. If a Black student engaged with them or tried to defend himself, the crooked wheels of justice conspired to blame the Black students, and they were expelled. Plĕas intervened. He knew just how to talk to the bastards and, if it wasn't resolved peacefully, he took it to a forest or a lot, and they settled things with their fists.

Plĕas respected anyone who had musical talent, sports abilities, or was just a high achiever. If he saw any bullies, White or Black, mess with anyone, he approached them and gave them a warning.

People learned not to mess with Plĕas. A good student who enjoyed being challenged, Plĕas was respected as a young man with an excellent eye for detail and a quickness with facts and problem-solving. By the time he graduated high school, he had a solid reputation as someone who had street smarts and book smarts.

The courage and determination he displayed in high school foreshadowed what Plĕas would do later in his life; fight for Black rights, and the integrity and preservation of his people's culture and right to ascend. His desire to intercede and make peace or defend those who couldn't defend themselves must have come from his father. Sadly, that character trait led to his father's death in a tragic incident when he tried to intercede in a knife fight on the way home

11

from work one night. Exactly what happened next is not known, but his body was found at the railway station the next day. His death was ruled an accident.

It was the same train station that sent forth locomotives carrying rich people who liked to stand on the platform and throw coins for the children to collect. As a child, Plĕas and the other children would run behind the locomotive to pick up the coins. Plĕas had a keen eye for the glint of sunlight on metal and collected a lot of money that way.

The death of Tusant Sr. was brutal to Plĕas and Johnnie because they were still very young, in elementary school. Plĕas was a few years older than Johnnie. Johnnie had such a strong-willed personality that Plĕas had to correct when he back-talked a few times to remind him that he was the boss while their father was on the road. Plĕas took his responsibilities seriously and couldn't wait to tell his father the things he took ownership of while he was away. When he helped his mother and brother, Plĕas felt like he was the family protector of the house until his father returned home.

The night they got the news about their father's tragic death, the family was devastated, and Plĕas felt he needed to get to the station the following day as early as possible. Once he arrived, he saw a man with a bucket of water who was cleaning off the blood from the platform. He sat on the bench located

12

on the platform for a few hours. It was so early in the morning that people hadn't arrived to take the local locomotive train to their next destination. It was perfect for Plĕas; it allowed him that time with his father's spirit and just thinking to himself that he would do everything in his power to keep the family together and make him proud of him.

I guess his father prepared him for this day and why he instilled in him and Johnnie the way of the world through his talks with them. His father talked with them with a loving heart, and no question they asked him was too silly. Plĕas loved that about his father whenever they had that father and son talk. Plĕas let the pain of his father's death give him strength, and he wore it with a badge of honor to represent his father in his glory. It was undoubtedly evident in his head that Tusant Sr. had no regrets about his actions. He tried to help solve a disagreement amongst two men; he lived by what he taught him, which also gave him peace.

However, his father's passing seemed to mark the end of his childhood, and the flipping and screaming sounds of a train that passed through now seemed to chant a new refrain in his father's voice: *"You're the man now, You're the man now. Always take care of your mama."*

Following her husband's untimely death, Bessie worked when she could, and Tusant's family sent her

13

money when times were tough, but it soon became apparent that it wasn't going to be enough. She needed to find a way to provide for her family. Bessie thoroughly considered her choices. Fortunately, she learned mindset and perseverance from her late husband.

There were few opportunities available to women in those days, and fewer still for Black men, but Bessie thought of a way. With the money her late husband left her, she decided to open a gentlemen's club, which later expanded to a juke joint; and turned the other house into a room and board. She found the perfect location for a classic juke joint across the tracks, at a rural crossroads on the outskirts of town, and designed her business to cater to the rural workforce.

Her business consisted of two shacks and one rowhouse, all situated next to one another. When she bought them, the shacks had good bones with cedar floors, and just needed to be painted and spruced up. Next, was them to be turned into comfortable, appealing gathering places where people could come to relax and socialize after a hard work week. She knew this was a much-needed enterprise during the era of Jim Crow, when most white establishments barred Black people.

Bessie soon proved herself to be a stern businesswoman who knew how to negotiate, shattering gender expectations and stereotypes decades before her time. When, for example, it came to getting supplies like lumber, nails, hammers, and other parts for her shacks, she never feared the white owners or suppliers. Instead, she approached them with confidence, and they respected her for it. When it was done, Bessie's place was elegant and filled with the fragrance of beautiful flowers, perfume, and great music. One shack was a room and board where guests could rest or stay over after they partied all night. The other half was a private club where traveling musicians could spend the night. When they weren't at school, Plĕas and Johnnie helped with chores, like sweeping, folding napkins, and straightened pushed-aside chairs.

Bessie's success instilled a sense of pride and self-confidence.

She had always wanted to be her own boss and realized this aspiration. Bessie also knew she provided a much-needed service for her community, which made Bessie feel like she was doing something worthwhile.

The women who worked for Bessie were warm and beautiful, and Bessie did her best to maintain a family atmosphere both for them and the boys, but she kept a pistol in her pocketbook, just in case. Plĕas said his mother told the women who worked for her,

"If you're going to get used by a man, you should get paid for it. Be your own businesswoman."

She also told them, "When these white men come in, or these out-of-towners, remember what they say." That way, if any of the white politicians or businessmen thought they were going to shut her down, she had some dirt on them. That knowledge gave her power. Bessie was a woman who acted like a lady but thought like a man. For a woman, her business savvy and entrepreneurship were unheard of, at the time.

Eventually, Bessie turned one of the other shacks into a juke joint and simple music hall with room for dancing and tables to enjoy food and drink. Half juke-joint and half jazz club, many of the musicians who came in performed just for the opportunity to receive a well-earned round of applause. On Saturday nights, word went out about who was to perform, and everyone turned up in their best dance clothes.

During this time, Bessie did her best to maintain a family atmosphere, and her house was clean and the boys well-mannered. Because Bessie treated the women who worked for her like family, Plĕas remembered them asking him how was school and made sure his homework was done? There were also strong male figures around, who taught Plĕas how to build and repair things. They also showed him how moonshine was made in a still, using corn as the primary source of fermentable sugar. In addition, those men made it clear that they wanted the boys to succeed and do well for themselves and gave them a pat on the head to show their affection. "It was a good feeling," he said. "A feeling of community."

Bessie's connections allowed her to help when the protests started. Many Black people knew there had to be a better way of life and they were determined to get it. They were sick of living with daily injustices and being treated like they were less than human. So, the last shack became a meeting place for protestors, where they discussed how to survive under Jim Crow. It was essential to address our rights. This was key for Bessie to find a way to move our people forward. She was of help when it came to food, and bail money; plus, if someone got hurt, she had a room for them to be taken care of; she had a white doctor on her payroll to help when she needed him. She used part of the money she made to support them in any way for this cause.

Even though they were loved and well-cared for, Emma, Bessie's mother, told her that this wasn't the right kind of atmosphere for Plĕas and Johnnie to grow up in, so she convinced Bessie to let them live with her. In later years, Plĕas recounted fond memories of the time he lived with his grandmother. He liked waking up and having breakfast as a family, going to school, and just feeling like a regular kid. Emma taught them basic manners, like putting their

toys away and standing up when adults entered the room. They enjoyed three delicious meals a day and could focus more on their schoolwork. While they lived with their grandmother, Plĕas first developed his love for cooking, as he went outside to pick the vegetables and helped her cook. Between the two households, Plĕas understood that book smarts and street smarts were equally important, and anyone who had one but not the other was nothing more than an educated fool.

Their grandmother was a religious woman. Plĕas remembered how she acted out the bible stories, changed her voice as she pretended to be each character. Plĕas loved that. It instilled in him the belief that you could be successful with the help of faith and prayer. Whenever he got worried or upset, she said, "Baby, you got to just give that up. Let God take care of that." That reassurance gave him a sense of confidence and security. They returned to living with their mother a few years later, but Plĕas remained a God-fearing man for the rest of his life.

Before they went back to Bessie's house, Plĕas' grandmother, Emma sat them down and told them some family stories she felt they needed to know to understand their mother. She told them that as Bessie grew up, she saw her mother get up at 5 A.M. to work for a white family and raised their children while raising her. She took three buses to get there and three to get back by 7 PM.

Thank God she had good neighbors that helped each other out when it came to monitoring the children while the parents had to work.

She'd seen a white man say to her father, "Boy, you hear me talking to you?" and felt the helplessness that all Black children felt as they witnessed what their parents endured.

Plĕas and Johnnie understood. They felt it themselves, but they lived in a time with a percolated promise for change. When they returned to Bessie's, her businesses had improved to a more professional clientele. Bessie missed her boys. She made sure they each had their own room and started doing more with them. She liked taking them to carnivals, throwing cookouts and birthday parties.

Settled in her business, she now had the freedom to focus on her boys and wanted them to have a good childhood.

Chapter 2
Meeting Lucille

Lucille Stone as a teenager

In 1940s Alabama, the civil rights movement burst upon the state like a pot of simmering grits forgotten on the stove. As Plĕas grew up, he listened to the protesters who stayed in one of his mother's shacks. They spoke of injustice and fighting the law with the law, but the more things stayed the same or got worse, their talk turned to taking it to the streets and fighting for their lives and rights. In Plĕas' heart stirred a passion for getting involved. He started joining protests outside of shops where Black people were kicked out and told, "Your money's no good here."

Plĕas thought, "Let them see how they do when none of us shops there!"

By this time, Plĕas had grown into a handsome young man, tall and thin like his father, with a flair for dressing well and famous for silencing any upstarts with his signature, cutting look. He was never a gangster, but he understood the street game and knew how to cut off a con before it happened.

His love for people and business prompted him to open pop-up party shacks for talent shows, dance contests, and musicians. He purchased folding chairs and tables, in addition to tablecloths and centerpieces. For Saturday nights, he charged a little more, because he added class and sophistication to the places. Ladies got dressed in their polka-dot circle or poodle skirts or tapered slacks with knotted, sweetheart, gingham-fitted tops and gloves. Men wore suits with wide-brimmed hats and shiny shoes. Everyone was happy to have a place where they met, partied and let off steam from a long, hard work week.

Jobs for Black people in the '50s were shining shoes, packing bags, chauffeuring cars, serving on railroads, and providing nanny, maid, butler, and cook services, etc. Young Black people who worked during the week wanted to spend some money on the weekends. With money, Black people were starting to flourish. When the work week was over, everyone just wanted to enjoy friends and family.

With some of the money they made, Plĕas and Johnnie slipped envelopes of cash into Emma's mailbox. They wanted to make sure she was able to wear beautiful fancy clothes and hats to church. They never forgot what she taught them and, on occasion, still sat in the back of the church to hear the preacher's sermon. After Emma died peacefully in her sleep, with a bible opened on her nightstand. Plĕas and Johnnie missed their grandmother dearly; so, did Bessie. But they never forgot what she taught them: get an education, because that is something no one can take away from you and keep God in your heart. Always.

At the parties, Plĕas used to see Lucille Stone—a 5'9", slim and chocolate young woman with long legs and a heart-melting smile. Lucille radiated confidence and style, and wore fine-looking clothes sewn for her by her mother and aunts. The flattering styles turned heads wherever she went.

Lucille and her cousin Clarence used to dance in the living room. They rolled up the rug and did the Jitterbug, the Lindy Hop, and the Hellzapoppin to the Cab Calloway Band music. They admired the Nicholas Brothers' tap and jazz moves. Lucille and Clarence signed up for any popular dance contest they could enter. She was a showstopper.

Even though she was five years his junior, Plĕas knew Lucille from high school and that she was a "good girl" from the right side of the tracks. She came to his dance contests with her cousin Clarence, and the two of them danced the jitterbug like nothing he'd ever seen. Clarence, a tall, light-skinned young man, was often shy until the music played. Then he threw Lucille around like a rag doll, and she didn't miss a beat, shaking her head and smiling wide to the rhythm of the music. Her sassy, sophisticated, and confident moves were a showstopper, and a perfect reflection of how she felt inside. When they danced, people cleared the dance floor, then stood around as they watched and cheered them on. Finally, Plĕas worked up the nerve to approach her.

He said, "Well, you keep winning all my money, so maybe we should start dating." Little did Plĕas and Lucille know, that their introduction created a long-lasting friendship.

Lucille introduced Plĕas to her mother Mary and brother Carter, a 6'4", dark-skinned and handsome young man who, despite being a lady-magnet, took his role as the family protector—following their father's death from pneumonia—seriously. Lucille, Carter, and their cousins were like siblings, but Carter was the anchor.

Carter Stone
Our Family Rock

Lucille knew the power of education. She was confident and had a sharp mind for business; she was a perfect fit for Plĕas, and he knew it. He pursued her passionately, called her every day and went to Sunday dinners at her family's home. At these dinners, Plĕas saw a different side of life; an intellectual environment where people agreed to disagree. Two people could look at the same matter, came to different conclusions, and they laughed and learned from each other. It was a refreshing change for Plĕas, who was used to people that competed to win an argument by cutting each other down and established who was right by any means. Lucille's house was filled with politicians, neighbors, the pastor, friends, and family. He never forgot the smells of glazed baked ham, lamb, fried chicken, collard greens, black-eyed peas, cornbread, and lemon pound cake that greeted him when he visited those Sunday afternoons. What a spread!

They weren't a wealthy family, just hard-working, respectable, church-going people who were educated and political. In contrast, Plĕas' family was focused on fast money and opportunities at any cost. For her part, Lucille was attracted to Plĕas' strong personality. She knew he was not the kind of man she could have controlled, which was fine with her, because she had her own goals in life. The world Lucille introduced

Plĕas to opened his eyes. Lucille liked him and wanted her family to accept him.

She instructed him, "When you come over to my family's house, don't wear those flashy clothes. You got to dress like you're going to church. And don't come empty-handed. Stop and get my mother or my grandmother flowers."

Plĕas was generally confident and entered a room like he owned it, but he had never seen such a feast or heard such civil and informative conversations. For the first time in his life, he was at a loss for words— just listened and absorbed the information imparted onto him by these educated people. He did his best to be perceived as worthy of Lucille and her family.

Lucille's family made it clear that she had to finish high school, and they approved of another boy she was dating, whose father was a lawyer and family was well-respected. So, Plĕas bided his time, stayed in touch with her and her family over the next five years. He knew he had to overcome his reputation and improve himself to win their approval; and was determined to do so. That included bettering himself personally and professionally. He began to understand that there was a better way to resolve problems than street fighting. It was more powerful to have confronted a problem with intelligence.

On the other side of the tracks, Bessie loved Lucille she thought Lucille was a ray of sunshine, and she really liked Lucille's 'sweet but don't take no mess from nobody' personality. Lucille, endeared herself to her future mother-in-law by doing Bessie's hair—something Lucille quickly discovered she had a talent for—and helped Bessie with her clothing styles. Very stylish herself, Lucille loved to read fashion magazines, and wasn't deterred by the fact that only white women were depicted on the cover. For her hair styles, Lucille used Madam C.J. Walker's hair products. Named for the inventor, Mrs. Walker was the first Black female millionaire, and everyone used at least some part of her "Walker System," which included hair grower, Glossine, and hot combs. The first day Lucille did Bessie's hair, Bessie insisted on paying. She gave her a *wash 'n set*, and Bessie exclaimed that she loved it. Lucille laughed and said, "You are my first paying customer."

It was the beginning of a regular weekend routine, where Lucille helped Bessie with her weekend outfits and did her hair. Lucille prided herself on the fact that her hairstyles lasted a week, and soon Bessie's friends started making hair appointments with Lucille as well. So, just like that, Lucille had a lucrative, part-time job. The two women gossiped, laughed and formed a lasting friendship that made Plĕas happy.

When Bessie passed away in 1951 at the age of fifty-six from complications of diabetes, she was surrounded by friends and family. Plĕas felt both sad and proud of the powerful woman who was before her time when women empowerment did not exist, a pioneer in women's entrepreneurship and activism. She was a trailblazer, a self-made woman who reflected, in her final moments, a fulfilled and productive life.

Chapter 3

Coming to Harlem

During this time, Plĕas began traveling between Birmingham and Harlem, New York, as a cook for the Seabo Railroad Company, where he further refined the cooking skills he learned from Emma and Lucille. His enthusiasm for cuisine and combining herbs and spices became his specialty. Unfortunately, incidents of racism were rising, with white supremacists harassing Black servers and workers, so the railway enforced policies and trained Black workers on their response. In this way, Plĕas was exposed to the racial injustices that happened not just in the South, but in New York, as well.

One of the stops on the railway line was Detroit, where Plĕas' Uncle Bob was the head of a syndicate that operated as street bankers, bookies, and protection providers; and sold items like television sets that, "fell off the back of the truck." In the streets, they had a hardcore reputation, but they were known to be fair. They used some of their money to help support their community, ensured people had what they needed, earned them emphatic nods of respect when they walked the streets. In addition, the women in the family ran legitimate businesses like hair salons and boutique clothing stores. "His family was so smooth," Plĕas used to say, "they should have been in politics."

Plĕas' Uncle Bob was a colorful character, reminiscent of Red Foxx from the movie "Harlem Nights," right down to the diamond pinky ring and fat cigar. His wife, Plĕas' Aunt Rose, was the spitting image of the movie character's wife, played by Della Reese. Rose was the heart and glue of the family. Plĕas visited them on these stopovers and became close with his cousins, who counted money and tallied the books faster than a calculator.

His cousin Penny was particularly adored by the community. With her big afro and bright eyes, she looked like the actress Pam Grier (also known as

Foxxy Brown). And, like the strong, street-smart, but also compassionate characters played by Grier, Penny was the one everyone talked to if they needed help or wanted a meeting with Uncle Bob. She organized community events and ensured that anyone who couldn't afford it, received a turkey with all the fixings for Thanksgiving or Christmas. Later in life, she continued to support the community by working with the city on community boards and organizations for thirty years.

Plĕas' brother Johnnie also came to Detroit, but unlike Plĕas, he met a woman and settled down there. He and his partner, Evelyn, had a baby girl named Pat, and they were the loves of his life.

During his free time, he repaired his motorcycle and rode it around and felt the fresh air that brushed against his face. However, his family wanted him to be mindful of the dangers of riding without that belt and helmet.

Tragically, when Pat was only a toddler, Johnnie died due to compound injuries sustained from riding his motorcycle without the supportive waist belt and helmet he was instructed to have on. Plĕas was so heartbroken because, even though they were brothers, once their father died early in their life, he felt that Johnnie was his responsibility. His death was something he could not have been shielded or protected from.

After his death, the Pearson's helped support Evelyn until she remarried years later and had two additional children.

For Plĕas, Detroit was a taste of home—his side of the tracks—and he started seeing Margaret, a woman he knew since his childhood visits to see his father's family in the summer. She was street smart and well respected. More importantly, the two of them had a powerful friendship but in a way that reminded Plĕas of Bessie; she was a strong, independent woman with a loving heart. When she got pregnant, she said, "I would never take you from Lucille. You can move on and get on with your life."

They had two boys together and maintained a loving and confiding friendship over the years, but she eventually met someone else, and Plĕas had his eyes set on moving to New York and a life with Lucille.

When Plĕas returned to Birmingham from his stays in Harlem, he told Lucille, "Baby, they're doing it up there in Harlem!"

In the '50s, Harlem was a mecca for Black people. The streets pulsed with the rhythm of soul, gospel, and R&B music. Successful Black people walked with confidence along 125th Street, past institutions like the Apollo Theater, Sugar Ray's, and the Palm Cafe. Children skipped rope, and women paraded in the latest fashions on the streets. Men exchanged gossip at the barbershop, and Black businesses were thriving everywhere. Plĕas knew he had to be a part of it.

Besides working on the railroad, Plĕas started working towards his dream by driving a cab in Birmingham during his layovers from the railway. He liked this idea because he got paid in cash and talked to customers, which allowed him to master his people skills. Financially, he did better than the other cab drivers because he figured out that he needed to go outside the regular routes and picked up wealthy customers from points where they entered Birmingham, starting with the railway stations. He took every opportunity to strike up a conversation with these customers and knew the right questions to ask to get them to talk about themselves. Those conversations were an education unto themselves, and Plĕas learned how a successful man thought, spoke, and acted. There was no color involved, just meaningful dialogue, laughter, and a meeting of intelligent minds. He asked them about their experiences and travels, which enriched his understanding of the world.

Plĕas learned from his successful customers how to negotiate. But how he looked was something he learned from his father, and he keenly observed and thought about how successful people presented themselves. So, he dressed with style and confidence and, over time, he formulated a trick of wrapping a hundred-dollar bill around a wad of ones or fives, which gave the illusion he was rolling. Plĕas saw life as a game in many ways, and he knew how to play it!

Black men grew up fast in those days. Due to the discrimination, they faced at every turn, success depended on learning how to make it at a young age. Plĕas had his sights set on a life with Lucille in Harlem, where he felt he had the opportunity to pursue his dreams without the discriminatory laws of Jim Crow. He was confident that he was up to the challenge. That confidence was, and always would be, rooted in home. He cherished the love he felt for his mother, Bessie, the wise and comforting teachings of Emma, and the warm embrace of his hometown Birmingham, Alabama. Those memories and experiences would continually light his way, as would his strong belief in God, which was his anchor. Additionally, he knew that his Detroit family was only a phone call away if he ever needed help.

On one of his layovers in New York, he decided to stay in Harlem for good and make it his home. He knew Lucille would graduate school soon, and he wanted to be ready for her. In those days, there were a lot of slum landlords in Harlem, but Plĕas kept his ears to the ground and found out that a bunch of buildings in Harlem were to get torn down in a few years so that the city could build housing projects. People displaced by the demolition would have priority for getting an apartment in the new buildings. So, he found a small apartment with a kitchenette in one of these buildings and made a living working as a cook at restaurants and doing odd jobs.

During his time off, he got to know the people in the community, the politicians, and business owners. On Saturday nights, he dressed up and visited the clubs or attended house parties. Sundays he went to church services and ate Sunday dinner in the basement assembly hall. He also participated in any protests going on in the street.

He visited Lucille on a few occasions, and they kept in touch with postcards and phone calls whenever possible. Plĕas squeezed into the telephone booth, placed in the hallway of his building and asked the long-distance operator to connect them. Eventually, he found out that the other boy her parents wanted for her, because he came from such a refined, successful family, got a girl pregnant after dropping Lucille back home after prom. Plĕas felt sorry her heart was broken but was also secretly relieved that his main adversary for Lucille's family's approval was out of the picture.

As happy as he was in Harlem, Plĕas kept his promise to her family and never influenced or told Lucille too much about his life in New York. When The St. Nicholas Housing Project opened in 1952, He was one of the first on the list after the war veterans and was given a two-bedroom apartment in building 240 perfect for him and Lucille (Later, when his family expanded, they moved to building 225). The site would eventually consist of four city blocks, with thirteen buildings between Seventh and Eighth Avenues and 127th and 131st Street.

The year before they moved into the new apartment, Lucille's mother and aunt found jobs as live-in maids on Long Island, New York. One weekend, when she had time off, Lucille's mother sent for her and her brother Carter to come up to New York for a family visit. She gave them instructions on how to get uptown and meet them on the steps of Salem United Methodist Church on 129th Street and 7th Avenue (now called Adam Clayton Powell Jr. Boulevard). Lucille's mother, Mary, picked Salem as their meeting place, because she knew it was a well-known landmark in Harlem.

The church has been a home and a sanctuary to many of the Harlem community and more, including singer Marian Anderson and poet Countee Cullen. Their Möller's Opus Organ's instrumental sound can be heard even outside of the church on Sunday mornings. As they waited, Plĕas happened to be walking back home down 129th street, carrying his groceries, when something told him to look up.

Plĕas and Lucille stared at each other, wide-eyed and speechless, then Plĕas ran across the street and picked her up, laughing as he swung her around, her straw hat falling to the ground and her crinoline skirt flying around her.

"I tried to write to you!" She said through her tears. "We were going to surprise you and invite you to dinner."

Plĕas hadn't received the letter, but nothing mattered now. He was hugging Lucille, and she smelled like home.

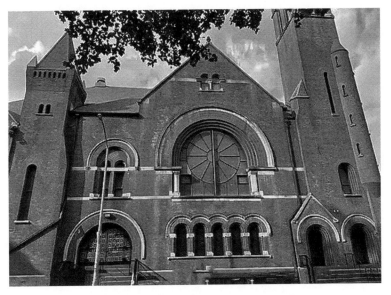

Salem United Methodist Church

Chapter 4
New Beginnings

Saint Nicholas Houses

Plĕas and Lucille were married in a small church ceremony in Birmingham, Alabama, on April 28, 1947, surrounded by their friends and family. Soon afterward, they took up residence at the St. Nicholas Houses in Harlem.

"St. Nick" was a beautiful housing development in its day, filled with a community of families who knew and cared for one another. Those lucky enough to have secured an apartment for themselves and their families felt proud and optimistic about the future. Outside, women sat on benches with their strollers. Teenagers played basketball in the big park. Other children played hopscotch, stickball, or skipped rope. There were playgrounds and tree-lined paths for biking, skateboarding, roller-skating, or for people who practiced their dance moves. Some women even started a flower garden in the center of the grounds. The warm, supportive community gave rise to many talented people and successful professionals, like singer-songwriter Teddy Riley, the music group Wreckx-N-Effect, R&B producer Patrick Adams, Billy Jones, The Sparks, The Soul Invaders, and many more.

At 131st Street between 7th and 8th Avenues, Mr. Donald Byrd's annual block party was an event to be remembered with music, games, and great food. The streets were blocked off to keep out the traffic, and Mr. Byrd put out folding chairs for the older folks to sit and enjoy the entertainment. In 2019, the St. Nicholas Houses Tenant Association added a "William Atmore Byrd Sr. Place" street sign under "Frederick Douglass Boulevard," to honor him and, fifty years later, "Old Timer's Day" is still a much anticipated and celebrated event to commemorate those wonderful block parties of yesteryear.

Harlem was bubbling with life and optimism. On the weekends, street performers lit up the corners along 125th street, and revolutionary speakers like Malcolm X spoke on civil rights messages outside the Theresa Hotel. Children clutched their mother's hands on their way to Buster Brown's where they bought shoes or shopped at Woolworth's or Blumstein's department store, the first store in the city to have a Black Santa Claus. Teenagers went to the arcade next to Lowe's Victoria Movie Theater to play games, and ate frankfurters and peanuts. Many still have the strip of photos taken in the arcade's photo booth, a treasured memento from a golden age.

On Saturdays in laundry mats, barbershops, and hair salons, gossip, jokes, and talk of politics rung in the air as everyone got excited for Saturday night. That was when people got dressed in their finest and went to the Apollo, the Cotton Club, or the Renaissance Casino and Ballroom to party and heard great music before they headed to Well's Chicken and Waffles or Small's Paradise on 135th Street.

At night, Harlem was a beautiful place where success and confidence filled the air. But no matter what you did on Saturday night, everyone got dressed in their Sunday best and went to church the following day.

The Shiloh Baptist Church, on 131st Street and Seventh Avenue, was a hubbub of activity on Sunday. During some weekends, they often had big revival tents set up outside, with live gospel music, choirs, food, and ushers in white suits and gloves to welcome patrons in and got a word of comfort, encouragement, and heard the word of God. The revivals successfully drew even more people into church on Sunday, where people listened to fiery sermons, heard great music, and enjoyed a meal downstairs. The third Sunday in September, congregants enjoyed the African Day Parade marching down the street as it passed the church. Afterward, people strolled along 125th Street to show off their Sunday best. These promenades were a sight to see on Easter Sunday with men, women, and children dressed in their fine Easter attire, reminiscent of a Fifth Avenue hat parade.

Lucille saw how Black people could live in a thriving, prosperous community for the first time. So, while Plĕas continued to work as a chef and in the print shop on the top floor of a department store (where he also printed political flyers after hours), Lucille got a job at Chock Full O'Nuts coffee shop and did women's hair in her apartment.

They were a popular couple and made friends easily. When they weren't working, they went to ballrooms, concerts, the community theater, parties, and events. At private parties, talk invariably shifted to discussions about racism, politics, and ways to protect Black interests and way of life. Plĕas listened with interest, and often took a lead in these discussions. His upbringing in Birmingham under Jim Crow taught him to be vigilant and aware. At the same time, he loved Black culture and entertainment, and spent many evenings and afternoons at the Apollo.

Between and after shows, he hung around to laugh and talk with the owners, entertainers, and crew—many of whom became important and life-long friends.

Plĕas and Lucille

Lucille got pregnant after three years of marriage, and the family was thrilled. Her grandmother, Frances Coats, quit her job as a maid to come live with them and take care of the baby. She was a proud, confident woman, yet too vain to wear the leg brace the doctors recommended. She walked with a slight limp, but her personality was so large that it was hardly noticeable.

Starting in the early '50s, the three Pearson children came into the world, and the growing family moved to a larger unit at St. Nick in building 225. Plĕas Tusant III—aka Sonny—was born first, then Larry three years later, and me, three years after that. Lucille stayed home with the children, and the Pearson household was a hubbub of activity at St. Nick. Whenever parents didn't know their children's whereabouts, they came knocking at Lucille's door. On rainy days the girls played with paper dolls made with clothes that Lucille snipped from fashion magazines and dressed on models she cut out of the tops of cardboard shoe boxes. The boys made handprints and figures out of Silly Putty, and they made baked apples and chocolate chip cookies.

In the early 1960s, Plĕas became president of the tenant's association. When the economy took a turn for the worse and people started losing their jobs, Plĕas convinced local doctors to waive or reduce their fees and provide medical assistance to the families in the St. Nicholas Houses. The doctors readily agreed when he pointed out that they would be getting patients for life. Then, after he worked out a deal with some local print shops, he printed 19,799 flyers for all the tenants. They read:

St. Nicholas Tenants Council Health Club

PLEAS T. PERSON,......President	HORACE ANITON,...... Fin. Secretary
FLOYD WEBB........Vice-President	PHYLISS MICHAELS...........Treasurer
ROSLYN GILLIAM...Rec. Secretary	ROSCOE JONES......Grievance Chr.
CARL COLEMAN......Legal Aid Chairman	

Dear Member:

This will introduce THE St. NICHOLAS HOUSING PROJECT HEALTH PLAN, endorsed by your President, P. T. Person and Officers of the Tenant's Council

A Membership Card will be given to you by your Officers. Don't Delay. Use it Today. Come to the Doctor's Offices for a Check-up

DOCTOR'S FEES
$4.00 Per Visit......Includes Injection
$5.00 Per X-Ray .....$2.00 Blood Test

HOURS:
Daily 1 to 8 P. M.
Thursday & Saturdays 1 to 6 P. M.

Yours for Good Health,

Pleas T. Person President
Roslyn Gilliam, Rec. Secy

50

If they heard someone was in trouble and in danger of being evicted, Lucille and Plĕas said, "That's not going to happen." So, they took up collections and negotiated payment plans with the rental office. Then they had the idea to organize rent parties, talent contests and shows to raise money. Plĕas stopped by WWRL/WLIB, the local radio station, and asked his disc jockey friends who attended and announced these events on the air, which promoted the parties. The African American Disc Jockeys and Black pioneers of radio in New York City like Frankie "Hollywood" Crocker, Eddie O'Jay and Hal Jackson were well-loved local celebrities, who promoted and made an appearance at the parties encouraged more people to come.

Other tenants were enlisted to help and collected donations. Lucille, her grandmother Frances, and Lucille's mother Mary organized the food, assembled a committee who went to local stores and asked them to donate food and beverages. Then she and some other tenants cooked meals. Everyone looked forward to the parties, which were hosted in the basement of Salem Church or the office community room at St. Nick. As a result of these efforts, the families who might have been kicked out were able to make arrangements with the management office to make payments on their rent until they got back on their feet.

Plĕas in front of Talent Show Sign

Justice for construction workers in Harlem

Then, construction was booming in Harlem, but the foremen at the construction sites insisted on hiring white workers and overlooked qualified Black men who needed jobs. White workers commuted into Harlem by train or drove in from Queens or Long Island along with out-of-state license plates to work on building sites in Harlem. Harlem residents felt the money from these projects should stay in the community. People talked about this injustice at gatherings and tenants' meetings in the community room at St. Nick. Plĕas heard the men say, "Man, they're building all around Harlem, and they don't want to hire any of our electricians or masonries. They look at us like we don't want to work." During those times, it was easier for Black women to get jobs, working in the office, housekeeping, and selling Tupperware or Avon.

The men made fun of the incompetence of the white workers on the site, who often asked the Black men around for help because they didn't know what they were doing. The white workers paid them back with lunch or a few dollars, but yet weren't hired.

Plĕas listened and said, "Let me look into that and see what I can do."

He put on a suit, went to the foremen, and said, "I'm representing the men in Harlem, and we want these men working. We've got skilled and licensed masonries and electricians."

He organized groups to scout out construction sites throughout Harlem—hundreds of men strong—and if a mason didn't show up, there was a Black man ready to take his place. Once on the job, they proved themselves to be effective workers. Plĕas printed signs from different printing shops, more than 50 Black men were assigned to different sites at a time from the Westside to the Eastside; throughout the years hundreds of men carried and demanded to be hired at each construction site. Plĕas said, "If you don't hire our men, we will shut you down." Men chanted slogans and asserted that this was their community and deserved to have the opportunity to build it up and profit from the work it entailed. The Black men in Harlem would not be disrespected. "We want to work; we are able to work. There is no need to totally import men into our community to build our community. It stops now!! We will picket every day, rain or shine."

At protests, Plĕas dressed modestly, with a black beret as a symbol of solidarity for the Black Panthers, while he muffled the outraged anger that burned from within. Each protest begun with a prayer of protection and victory. He reminded himself and the men with him that they were fighting for a higher purpose; the right to work, be free to prosper, and have control over their lives. Often, the police tried intimidation tactics amongst the protesters as they slowly drove by in their patrol cars or walked close to them. But they held the line, convicted that their cause was both just and righteous.

Plĕas and his men marched on sites all over Harlem. "We're not asking for handouts," he said. "These are skilled workers, and they have the right to work."

He would say to the foremen: "You have a vacancy there? Okay, we'll fill that job slot, but then you have to take two skilled workers on the payroll."

To his supporters, he forewarned: "We have to protect ourselves now. When you see outside developers scamming and building in our community, you have to act now. Otherwise, people will be priced out of their own neighborhood."

The protests Plĕas organized were peaceful. He told his men that if they had any weapons, they needed to be tucked in the cooler under the lunch table he had set up because he didn't want any violence. "Never be afraid to fail," he said. "Because you're just learning how to win."

Plĕas also went to the Department of City Contracts and researched the ins and outs of new construction projects, health and safety regulations, and labor laws. Then he made a list of categories: engineers, plumbers, masons, etc., and organized meetings to educate the men in Harlem about the requirements and processes of getting hired. Captains were put in charge of each field of specialty and got people employed in that area. Plĕas also attended meetings for the NAACP, the National Urban League, and the Democratic Club to spread the word about what he was doing, make connections and gained support. Each day they marched and protested. When people got arrested, Plĕas used his new connections to get them out.

But he knew the cops who got in their faces when they chanted "Shut them down!" were on the payroll of the real estate developers, and it seemed like no matter what he did, they were committed to getting him and his men arrested. Plĕas' activism had a cost: he was now on the radar of the white cops who were determined to bring him down.

Franklin Delano Roosevelt Jr.,
shaking hands with Plĕas T. Pearson

At a planning meeting in midtown Manhattan, Plĕas overheard three distinguished-looking white men discussing ways to help the Black community. He introduced himself and explained that Black men weren't looking for a handout; they just wanted job training so they could make their own living. They said, "Why don't you come down to our planning committee next week? You can tell us what you're doing and what is your vision for helping the Harlem community."

It turned out that two of those men were none other than two former United States Presidents' sons, Franklin Delano Roosevelt Jr., son and namesake of the venerable President who had struck a New Deal for suffering American families during the Great Depression, and Vice President John Davison Rockefeller Jr.'s son. Plĕas attended the meeting, and although he understood that their motives were not entirely altruistic—helping Black people and investing in their causes was an automatic tax write-off and benefited their reputations enormously and, it even looked better if they helped minorities during this time of rioting and fighting for justice and job opportunities. Plĕas realized that if white guilt worked in his favor, he ought to make some use of it!

Plĕas shared this opportunity with Lucille because she really was a visionary person and had a sharp mind for business. He knew her advice and opinion was invaluable to him. They kept this idea to a small network of people, close to the vest, so they could approach it in the right way and not blow this fantastic opportunity.

Determined and motivated, Plĕas set his mind towards doing everything he could to help the men and women of Harlem get job training and opportunities. Only God could have put the right man in the right place to have accomplished what he did. He knew he could not squander the opportunity of the financial gifts from these wealthy philanthropists, and further proposed to these supporters that the effort needed to include stipends for people while they received job training. He reached out to business owners so they would be ready to hire the newly qualified workers once their training was completed. Plĕas invited various Black business owners and politicians and lawyers who helped structure his proposal and presented it at a meeting, where he explained that this program not only allowed Harlem residents to earn a fair wage that provided for their families, but those who participated came away with a marketable skill and related experience to be used anywhere in the world.

Soon, bi-weekly meetings were arranged, where investors and participants gave updates on the progress of the proposal's status. At one of these meetings, a young philanthropist said, "Think as big as you can while the money is there." Determined to do just that, Plĕas reached out to Black organizations in the Harlem community, explained his mission and asked for their input and support, which ensured a collective, beneficial outcome. He diligently considered every angle then devised a budget that ensured both the training coaches, trainees, and job placement officers got paid. In his proposal, he also included additional training in office skills and general business operations.

It was also a weighted task to have designed the courses themselves. Plĕas' courses included cross-training some of the construction workers and other workers—male and female—in both manual labor, book-keeping, profit and loss calculations, and

Franklin Delano Roosevelt Jr. with Plĕas T. Pearson

general office skills, which gave them every opportunity to be hired in some capacity.

Plĕas understood that the payback for this generosity was political support for the supporters, and he was happy to give it. Back in the '60s and '70s, Black people had to discern which candidate would keep their promises and help their community. Roosevelt's

*Plĕas Pearson shaking hands with
John Davison Rockefeller Jr .*

generosity and support ensured him the Black vote in Harlem, because he was running for Senate.

With the donated money, Plĕas took over a few floors in the Theresa Hotel, where he ran workshops and job training programs. As promised, Plĕas promoted their political endeavors and spread the word, got the people to vote, and had set up voter registration tables at the weekly community meeting.

The training program helped hundreds of people in Harlem. Established as a grant program, Plĕas made sure it was well-stocked with office and classroom supplies and was proud of his success, because he got decent people into proper jobs. Plĕas never cared about publicity, just that he got people employed; but he felt gratified every time someone was successful due to his efforts.

Plĕas prided himself on investing in people. He knew his grandmother would have been proud of him because she always told him to stop thinking about what was in it for him, and to feel the empowerment of doing something to have elevated someone else's life for the better.

This opportunity to educate his people gave Plĕas an amazing feeling. Years later, when he visited Harlem, he told people who needed help getting a job to go to the Theresa Hotel and tell them at the office that Plĕas sent them. "And, when you get the chance, let me know how they treated you." To Plĕas' surprise, when they used his name, they were well respected; that was like money in the bank to him.

Plĕas was given an award for his involvement by various organizations.

The struggle to get Black representation in the planning of building up and the modernization of Harlem was something Plĕas continued to advocate for throughout his life. The injustice of white people getting loans to build in Harlem when Black people, who met the same financial prerequisites, were refused bothered him deeply. He knew that white people would return to Harlem one day, and the neighborhood would be gentrified.

If we had the opportunity, Black people, he said, would have attended the board meetings and would have perused the infrastructure plans for urban planning in Harlem. After all, he said, you wouldn't have developed Little Italy without having Italians on the planning commission or working on the construction site; or expand a Jewish neighborhood in Brooklyn without Jewish people who contributed their opinion on how that should have proceeded. He wanted to make a policy whereby developers had to hire from the community if they wanted to build in Harlem. Sadly, such a policy was never passed, and today, longtime Harlem residents are being forced out of the community as rents are increased by twenty to twenty-five percent.

Adam Clayton Powell Jr.

Adam Clayton Powell Jr., in the center,
back left of Plĕas Pearson

Another cherished political connection of Plĕas' was Adam Clayton Powell Jr., a Baptist pastor who became the representative of Harlem in the United States House of Representatives from 1945 to 1971. Young people living in Harlem today may stroll down Adam Clayton Powell Jr. Boulevard (formerly Seventh Avenue) or pass by his statue on 125th Street and not appreciate what a powerful personality he was for Black people in the 1940s and '50s. Powell was a pioneer in civil rights protests in New York, organized picket lines as far back as 1939 at the World's Fair headquarters in the Empire

State Building, which demanded that Black people be hired to work at the momentous site. His efforts resulted in a dramatic increase in Black labor. Adam Clayton Powell Jr. decided to run for New York's 16th district U.S. House of Representatives seat around 1952. When Plĕas had available time, he helped Adam with the campaign. However, Adam Clayton Powell Jr. was already protesting and picketing in downtown areas, which was the opportunity Plĕas wanted to have open as well. Adam's liked Plĕas' strategical plan for action, and his publicity tactics were powerful, effective, and applicable to different future situations. Plĕas thought about the details and planning needed to get the maximum results.

Powell encouraged Plĕas with his idea to take his fight downtown to the head offices of the planning and development committees. He said, "Tell them if there are not any Black men being hired, you'll shut them down." Those institutions didn't want the publicity and uptown white workers started to take other jobs rather than cross Plĕas' picket lines. In the end, their perseverance won out.

Chapter 5

Private Car Service and The Chat 'N Chew Restaurant

Plĕas and Lucille shared a love and talent for cooking, and in the early years of their marriage, they had an opportunity to open a soul food restaurant in Brooklyn. In Manhattan in the 1950s and '60s, bars closed at midnight, and it was almost impossible to find a restaurant open after 10 PM. But the rules were different in Brooklyn, where restaurants could stay open until 1 AM. So, when they heard that a building was available in the historic district of Bedford-Stuyvesant, they jumped on the opportunity and opened the *Chat 'N Chew Restaurant.*

Plĕas had the novel idea to put a hole in the wall above the door with a big fan to disperse the delicious cooking smells outside and draw customers in. He also had the construction workers put in a big, plate

glass window so that passers-by could see the ribs and chicken roasting on the open pit. The ideas worked, and soon after they opened, there were lines of people snaking down the block and around the corner, who waited to get in.

Two private rooms in the back were for celebrities and band members or private diners, an idea Plĕas got from his mother, Bessie. Lucille, who'd always dreamed of owning a brownstone in Harlem with a supper club (and a day spa on the second floor) realized her dream at least partially, with the new restaurant. She infused it with her personality, charm, and decorating skills. The restaurant quickly became the go-to spot for celebrities and partiers, who raved about the great food and atmosphere. The venture was a terrific success for five years, but after that the landlord lost the building, so Plĕas and Lucille had to give up the lease. It was a great thing while it lasted, but Lucille was tired by the end and realized she wanted to dedicate herself more to raising her children. So, it was on to the next venture for Plĕas!

Recent photo of Apollo Theater

Private Car Service

As he hung out at the Apollo Theatre in the 1950s and '60s, Plĕas noticed that the entertainers just barely made it on time to their performances because regular cab services, like yellow cabs, refused to go to Harlem. During that time, people used to "play the numbers." Back in the day, before the government took over—supposedly to raise money to improve the schools—local bookies made a living by running the numbers, taking people's orders at barbershops, stores, and bars. Plĕas always played the numbers 240 and 225, his building numbers at St. Nick.

One day, his numbers came in, and he knew exactly what he would do with the money. He combined it with some capital he had saved in the bank and started a private car service to bring entertainers and others to Harlem. He became one of the first licensed, Black-owned limousine and gypsy cab driver services in New York. He bought a tan Dodge car and then a few limousines. While the exterior of the Dodge was unassuming, inside it was furnished with top-of-the-line amenities. When he picked entertainers up from the airport, they got in the Dodge. The limousines acted as a decoy, with fully dressed chauffeur attire. Nobody ever imagined that A-list celebrities would had arrived in a tan Dodge, so they thronged the limousines, hoping for a glimpse of their favorite star. Meanwhile, Plĕas quietly drove the stars to a back entrance so they could slip in without being mobbed.

The clever ruse meant that Plĕas' high-end clientele made it to their sold-out performances on time, without being obstructed by their eager fans. His clients promptly told the Apollo's owners how helpful and stress-free Plĕas' service was for them. Impressed with Plĕas' ingenious idea, they established a business relationship with Plĕas, and he was regularly contacted to chauffeur celebrities to the Apollo. Additionally, he drove them to meetings, television appearances, radio engagements, recording studio sessions, and the like.

The Theresa Hotel (The Waldorf of Harlem & Theresa Towers)

Plĕas was proud to tell people that he was a private chauffeur for the Apollo. As his business expanded, he opened an office at the Theresa Hotel on 125th Street—a beautiful hotel in its grander days, it was known as the "Waldorf of Harlem." The interior had red carpeted stairs from the top to the bottom, a grand entrance with doormen, royal service, restaurants, a newspaper stand in the lobby, beautiful elevators, reasonably sized rooms, and completely breathtaking views. The exterior façade was white terra cotta and brick that created a distinctive structure that can be seen for miles.

Soon Plĕas had enough people that worked for him that he was free to attend anti-segregation and civil rights protests out of town, including Martin Luther King's famous March on Washington. Plĕas brought his son Larry on his tenth birthday, an unforgettable experience of a lifetime for the young boy.

He hired staff, including a receptionist who answered multiple calls on a console phone line. The phone lines were divided into celebrities' requests and new and local customers. The hotel, which was constantly filled to capacity, also became part of his clientele that expanded his business even more. Guests were thrilled that their hotel package included a car service.

While he was on the road, Lucille found a way to make extra money when she cook Saturday dinners with her grandmother. She started sending plates over to the Apollo, and the entertainers couldn't get enough of her delicious dishes. Her food was so popular that entertainers put their orders in before they got on the plane to come to New York. Larry and Sonny delivered the meals. She had a standard menu and, of course, she took special orders for fish sandwiches on Fridays. They cost $2.50, and her dinners were $5.00—that was a lot of money for a dinner during those times. A basic dinner anywhere else would have been about $3.00. Lucille thought like a businesswoman who had expenses; she was a mother and wanted to help bring in money to the household to stretch their income.

On the menu: fish and chips, black-eyed peas, collard greens, fried chicken with biscuits, and homemade banana pudding were all popular items.

When Plĕas picked entertainers up at the airport, they asked, "Do you know where I can get a meal around town?"

Plĕas answered, "Yeah, my house."

And so, the residents of the St. Nicholas Houses saw some famous entertainers cross their courtyard and take the elevator up to Plĕas' apartment to have one of Lucille's meals.

Along with the meals, Lucille styled hair and gave facials in the apartment, which supplemented her income. Lucille stopped selling dinners around Eastertime because she was booked with children's and adult's hair appointments. She styled my hair in Shirley Temple curls, since I had shoulder-length hair. Lucille wore her hair in a French roll. She even offered to do different hairdos at a reasonable price.

Then, in the mid-60s, she enrolled in Apex Beauty School on 135th Street and was so good at hairstyling that she got calls from the fabulous dancers at the Apollo to do their hair before the shows. Eventually the school asked her to be an instructor. When Black women still didn't have many opportunities, Lucille was founding her way and gaining a sense of independence and confidence.

When Lucille finally found out about Plĕas' relationship with Margaret and the boys they had together, she came to terms with it, and the two boys—now teenagers—came to visit one summer. With their edgy Detroit flash, and movie-star good looks, they were a hit with the girls at St. Nick, and the children formed a bond that continued throughout their lives. But Lucille was gaining an understanding that Plĕas' life outside their apartment might include more than politics, chauffeuring, and protests.

Chapter 6
Powerful Leaders in
Their Own Right

Both through his activism on behalf of the construction workers, and his limousine service, Plĕas became even more well-known and respected in the community, and was a trusted friend and confidant to many celebrities. He knew Malcolm X from the community, and whenever they saw each other, they greeted one another with a hug or a handshake. Malcolm X also acknowledged Plĕas' contribution to the community. Plĕas got him an office at the Theresa Hotel, they had regularly talked about the changes they were both trying to make in Harlem, to benefit the community. When Plĕas protested, Malcolm X came out to support him, and when Malcolm X had a protest or gave a speech, Plĕas reciprocated. They both understood street culture, and their mutual commitment for improved conditions for the people of Harlem resulted in a warm friendship of mutual respect.

Muhammad Ali (then named Cassius Clay) heard about Plĕas and started using his car service. The two developed a friendship, and Plĕas talked to him about his protests for the construction workers and kept him up-to-date with all the empowerment projects that occurred in Harlem. Ali saw how people respected Plĕas. Everyone from street hustlers to churchgoers and successful businesspeople acknowledged him with a respectful handshake. Plĕas drove him to some of his radio show appointments and to places where he could show his love for Harlem. Muhammad Ali drew crowds and the people used to go crazy when he said, "I am the greatest. I said that even before I knew I was". The people of Harlem were so proud of him, Muhammad Ali had no problem standing on 125th Street and taking pictures or giving out autographs.

Twenty years Plĕas' junior, Muhammad Ali came to look up to Plĕas and valued his advice. Ali used Plĕas' business services for a brief period, and Plĕas' receptionist reached out to Howard Bingham to give him the messages that came in for Ali. Plĕas got him an office next to him and Malcolm X where he could receive fan mail and hold press conferences. Plĕas became a trusted confidant to Ali, and even went over his travel itineraries, ensuring he had enough time to rest and eat. He was aware that Plĕas knew New York City best.

Malcolm X (left), Muhammad Ali (center),
Plĕas Pearson (right)

Ali liked the fact that Plĕas was a possibility thinker and appreciated the advice he gave, and also the fact that Plĕas had some thug in him, which gave him an edge. With Plĕas, people knew that if you had a beef with him, you had one chance to back your shit up, and then it was his turn. Ali observed how people respected that about him. For his part, Plĕas never betrayed a confidence, and Ali knew he could tell Plĕas anything and asked his advice on professional agreements or personal matters. Plĕas would always give him his honest opinion, sprinkled with his characteristic optimism and positive attitude.

Howard Bingham was the photographer who took some of the best pictures of Muhammad Ali during that time. Howard and Plĕas developed a friendship soon after Ali introduced them. Ali wanted Plĕas to get together with them going forward. Whenever Ali was touring, he took Howard Bingham with him, and whenever Plĕas saw a good photo of Muhammad Ali in a newspaper or magazine, he called Bingham and they laughed and talked about what was going on when the photo was taken.

On the day of this historical photo, there were a few other photos taken. Muhammad Ali, Howard, Malcolm X, and Plĕas had some scheduled meetings but wanted to walk through the streets of Harlem. Howard caught their every move.

Howard Bingham's exclusive photo landed in the major papers. Little did Plĕas know, his image appeared on the front of the Daily News and many other newspapers around the world. Even though that photo was taken more than fifty years ago, it still played an incredible role in history. There were a few of these photos with Plĕas Tusant Pearson, Malcolm X, and Muhammad Ali together at different locations during that day.

During Muhammad Ali's funeral service on June 10, 2016, CNN displayed that same photo of the three of them while Actor/Comedian Billy Crystal made his heartfelt speech about his friend, Ali.

This biographical book, *For the Strength of Harlem*, was written to add some clarity to that. For many years, people just knew Plĕas as "the man in the middle." However, he had to have some significance to these two legendary men, and it was important to tell why he appeared in that photo.

Joe Louis—aka "The Brown Bomber"

Joe Louis—aka "The Brown Bomber"—was another boxer-friend of Plĕas. He and Plĕas knew each other from their formative Detroit days. There they experienced good and bad times, and both understood the struggle of being a Black man in America. This was before Louis became an American hero, after he defeated heavyweight Max Schmeling, precipitating one of the biggest parties in Harlem when he became the world's heavyweight champion. As Paul Robeson sang in "King Joe," a famous song about the event by Richard Wright and William Basie: *"I've been in Cleveland, St. Louis, and Chicago too. But the best is Harlem when a Joe Louis fight is through."*

Joe and Plĕas got back in touch in New York when they each heard of the other's commitment to improving the employment situation for Blacks in Harlem. Joe started using Plĕas' car service and as they got to know each other again. Joe wanted to contribute to worthy causes in Harlem, so he gave Plĕas money and asked him to take it to non-profit organizations that needed support. Over time, they got so close that when Joe wasn't available to accept an award, he asked Plĕas to go to the ceremony and receive it on

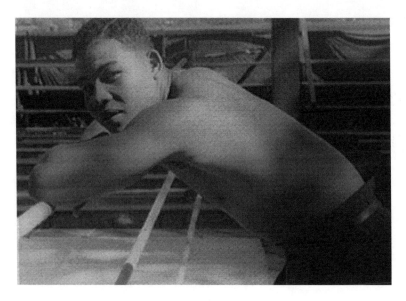

his behalf. Plĕas was honored and touched to do this for his old friend, as he prepared for his next fight. Plĕas felt being asked to represent his old friend was as much of an honor as to have received an award himself. The photograph below depicts Plĕas as he accepted an award for Joe at the Uptown Chamber of Commerce in Harlem.

Once two edgy youths on the streets of Detroit, Joe and Plĕas followed different paths, yet arrived at the same critical juncture in Black history and were brothers in their fight for civil rights in Harlem and across the country.

Nat King Cole

When the famous singer Nat King Cole came to
New York City, Plĕas received a call from his manager.
He picked Nat up at the airport and brought him to
the Theresa Hotel, but remained available for the du-
ration of Nat's stay in NYC. Nat, most famous for songs
like "The Christmas Song," *(easily recognized with the
beginning lyrics: Chestnuts roasting on an open fire...)*
and "Unforgettable," was also the first Black man who
hosted an American television show when he premie-
red "The Nat King Cole Show" in November 1956. During his career, he recorded over one hundred songs,
many of which topped the pop charts. He often came
to New York City where he performed or appeared on
a network or at the Apollo. Nat wanted to hear about
Plĕas' endeavors on behalf of the Black community, as
well as spread some money around the neighborhood
and explored the different restaurants and clubs in
Harlem.

Over the years, the two enjoyed a close friendship.
One day, when Nat was to perform on an evening television program, he called Plĕas to drive him to the
station and bring him back uptown afterwards. On that
particular morning, both Nat and Plĕas has decided to
get their hair done. Both men liked the "process cork,"
a fashionable hairstyle for Black men from the 1920s
through the 1950s. It was a straight, slicked-back look

with waves and was considered very fashionable. The two men walked into the barbershop together. When Nat King Cole entered the crowded barbershop, everyone was impressed that the famous singer was right there, at Roger Simon's barbershop in Harlem on 7th Avenue, between 123rd and 124th Streets.

Noting their reaction, Plĕas laughed and said, "No way is Nat getting his process done before me just because he's some big star! So, Mr. Movie Star, you can have a seat and wait your turn."

Plĕas told their barber he was a regular customer, and the barber chuckled because Plĕas was right. He tipped big, too!

Everyone in the shop laughed because it was true. Plĕas was a regular customer. It all worked out.

Nat said, "Plĕas, that's why I like you, man. You are all right with me. Now let's get some lunch."

He shook his head and smiled. That was a routine they had done before; it was really for a good laugh at the barbershop.

After they both got their hair done, they went to a restaurant to have lunch and then went to Nat's television performance.

The interaction was typical for the barbershop/beauty salon culture of most Black communities, where people discussed politics, sports, health, family, and community matters. These institutions were part of the fabric of Harlem, and Black culture all over the country. Saturdays were most busy, but on any given day, it was a sanctuary within the community; where barbers and stylists created unique bonds with their customers. For many, the crowd at the barbershop was a second family and Black men and women always walked out with the latest hairstyles.

Second to the right James Howard Meredith,
Drew "Bundini" Brown (center), Plĕas Pearson (right)

James Meredith

Plĕas' friendships ranged from struggling families to movie stars and politicians. Along with the rest of Harlem, he was delighted when the famous civil rights activist, James Meredith, came to the neighborhood in 1962, and Plĕas got to meet him personally. Fresh on the heels of a historic march in Mississippi, Meredith came to Harlem, encouraged education and voter rights. In a famous photograph taken during the visit, Plĕas is seated at the table with Meredith and Drew

"Bundini" Brown, the famous lyricist who wrote one of Ali's most famed refrains: ***"Float like a butterfly, sting like a bee. Your hands can't hit what your eyes can't see."***

Like Ruby Bridges, Meredith broke the color barrier at the University of Mississippi in 1962 with the aid of the National Guard, who had to fend off the hordes of white protesters who blocked him. He graduated in 1963 with a degree in Political Science and went on to lead the famous "March Against Fear" from Memphis, Tennessee, to Jackson, Mississippi. He was shot on the second day by a white gunman but recovered in time to join the protesters for the final journey, as they entered Jackson on June 26, 1966. Approximately 15,000 protesters participated in the march, making it one of the largest civil rights protests in the South, and inspired further activism and voter advocacy.

It seemed that things were looking up for the Black community at times. But, like Meredith, Plĕas' activism had earned him the ire of the police, who harassed him at every opportunity. He was followed everywhere, and cops tried to pick a fight with him so he would react, giving them an excuse to arrest him. Eventually, it got so bad he had to move.

Some friends found him an apartment near Lincoln Center on Manhattan's west side and, despite his reluctance to move away from his community, Plĕas realized he didn't have a choice. Living in a building with an eclectic group of artists and professionals exposed Plĕas' to a new world of possibilities and interests. His horizons were broadening, and, lived away from Lucille, the two drifted apart.

It was a man's world back then, and relations between Plĕas and Lucille were becoming strained. In general, she felt he wasn't there for her when she needed him. She improved herself, regained her self-esteem and enrolled in a nursing assistant program. Eventually, she landed a position at the Presbyterian Hospital on 168th Street in the Washington Heights neighborhood of Upper Manhattan. She was excited about this new chapter in her life and felt like she could take care of herself.

One day, as I walked with her to the grocery store, and pushed the shopping cart down 129th street— ironically the same street she and Plĕas reunited on the steps of the Salem Church decades earlier—she said, "I'm gonna talk to you about something, okay? You know, your dad loves you and I love you. But your father and I, we've had our worries—we have our problems. We all love you kids, and your father is always going to be your dad." She paused before continuing in a sarcastic tone. "But you know, he don't always have to be my husband."

Even though they already lived separately, I was worried I wasn't going to see my father anymore. But my mother reassured me, saying, "We both love you, and your father's gonna take you every two weeks."

The end of Lucille's marriage to Plĕas was undoubtedly the end of an era, but the couple stayed close, and their relationship actually improved after the divorce. Plĕas came to Sunday dinners, and the two remained friends.

Chapter 7
Travel and Food Go
Hand in Hand

Pleas wanted to learn to speak and understand different languages, primarily because outside store owners—mainly Jewish, Italians, and Spanish—were doing business in Harlem. He attended the Synagogue with a community of Ethiopian Jews in Harlem, the

"Royal Order of Ethiopian Hebrews." A devoutly religious man, who knew how to read the Hebrew alphabet and being exposed to Jewish culture inspired Plĕas. Nevertheless, he had a deep respect for other religions and cultures and appreciated what they could teach him.

When he was on the Lower East Side, he liked to go to Katz's Delicatessen and get matzo ball soup and pastrami sandwiches. The owners loved Plĕas, and he would often sit and talk to the regulars, who taught him to speak Yiddish. He was so quick with learning that he soon conversant. A devoutly religious man, Plĕas nevertheless had a deep respect for other religions and cultures and appreciated what they taught him.

The neighborhood was populated with people from diverse backgrounds and a variety of countries and, in an effort to learn the language, Plĕas instructed the local grocery-store owner to say the Spanish name for each item as he placed it in the bag. He also made efforts to learn some Greek and French and got so proficient that he jumped into people's conversations speaking in their native language, giving everyone a shock, followed by a good laugh. Besides language, food, he felt, was the common denominator and a defining characteristic of each culture. When he got the travel bug, he made an effort to learn the language of the countries where he intended to travel and visited restaurants in New York that featured their cuisine. In addition, learning how other cultures combined herbs and spices allowed him to expand his cooking repertoire, and he learned to incorporate those techniques into his own recipes.

Paul Robeson, the famous actor, musician, and activist well-known for singing "Old Man River" in the 1936 movie "Show Boat," used to say to Plĕas, "You gotta go over to Europe. You gotta get out of the United States just to see what it feels like." He also told him that he could only taste the authentic food of a culture if he visited the country.

Plĕas met a travel agent. While they were talking, he noticed she had an accent. He asked her what her ethnicity was. After he told her of his desire to travel, she told him about a group going to Brazil in two months and asked if he wanted to join the traveling group. This gave him the opportunity to travel internationally with an experienced and knowledgeable group of travelers going to Brazil. The experience was transformative. It opened his mind to a new way of life. After that, he went to the Bahamas and several European countries. Along the way, he sent postcards back to people in Harlem.

When he was abroad, people asked him about his hometown. Plĕas was only too happy to oblige and told them about his village, "sweet, sweet Harlem." Where the famous Langston Hughes, Countee Cullen, Duke Ellington, Lena Horne, and so many more lived. He told them how he fought for the strength of Harlem and the struggles of Black people, but he also focused on what a wonderful community he came from.

In the '60s and '70s, Harlem was bustling with an innovative R&B music scene, children jumped through fire hydrants retrofitted with sawed-off soda cans, independent store owners sold dashikis and incense, iconic, natural afros, Power to the People, and the booming refrain of James' Brown's "Say it Loud – I'm Black, and I'm Proud." On the weekends, families packed picnic lunches and went to Randall's Island Park, where they barbequed, jumped rope, played cards, and enjoyed the beautiful view of the Manhattan skyline. He described the music and the block parties, stickball, and double-Dutch, 125th Street, and the big, extended family at St. Nick.

They delighted in hearing his descriptions of the barbershops where men "kicked it" and talked about everything from politics to the fine-looking women they admired, and the beauty salons where women gossiped and laughed while they got their hair done. He described the street musicians and the department stores, like Woolworths, Ronnie Casuals, AJ Lester's where you got tailor-made suits and with its fancy hat displays, and Florsheim, where you could have bought a fine pair of men's shoes.

And he told them about the fantastic nightlife: the Apollo, the Cotton Club, the Savoy Ballroom, and the Paris Blues Jazz Club. There was the Red Rooster, the historic district dubbed "Strivers Row," and the Renaissance Casino and Ballroom, where men in tuxedos and women in ball gowns danced the night away. There was so much to tell, and Plĕas delighted in telling it. As much as he loved to travel and admired so many things about the countries he visited, his experiences abroad just made him appreciate home all the more.

Plĕas continued to work as a chef at hotels, restaurants, clubs, and for celebrity clients. His association with the Apollo had earned him enough contacts that he always had a job someplace. Plĕas'

Chef Plĕas T. Pearson

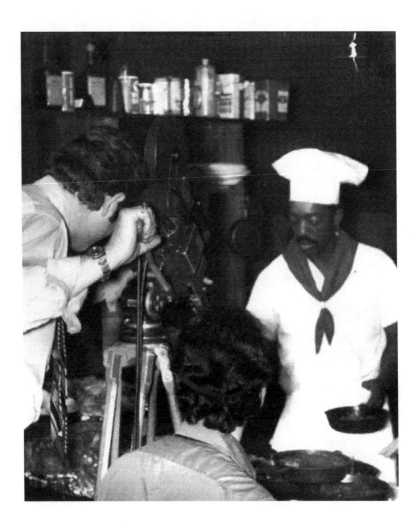

world broadened beyond the eclectic group of people he got to know at his new building.

Back on West 68th street, one of Plĕas' new neighbors told him with his cooking skills and experience, he was qualified to get more prestigious chef jobs. She offered to optimize his resume to reflect his international experience and changed his title to "Chef and Restaurant Connoisseur." As a result, he got better-paying jobs at The Sheraton Hotel, the Copacabana restaurant at 10 E 60th Street, Hilly's in the West Village—a trendy spot with folk singers and open mic night—and Central Park's famous Tavern on the Green.

In those days, when people enjoyed their meal, they would ask to meet the chef. Plĕas was complimented for his innovative cooking and, when he came out to greet these customers, he used to say, "Do you have a business card?" When they handed it over, he laughed and said, "All right, now you're my reference."

One day the crew from a popular morning show came in for lunch at Tavern on the Green and asked to meet the chef. One of the men couldn't believe what he'd done with a traditional dish, still maintained its integrity, but added innovative seasoning and presented the meal in such an elegant fashion. Plĕas came out, shook their hands, and discussed his recipes with them, which were featured as the "specials of the day."

A short time later, when Plĕas worked at Hilly's, a trendy, "go-to" restaurant in Greenwich Village, the same crew came to dine and when they tasted the food, one of them said, "I know this style of cooking!" They asked if they could give their compliments to the chef and were happily surprised when Chef T. Pearson walked out again! They knew that this was providence, and Plĕas needed to come on the show. A few weeks later, the crew arrived with lights and cameras and Plĕas became one of the first Black chefs to be featured on a morning talk show. His reputation for delicious dishes got a lot of buzz in the restaurant business. In the segment, he demonstrated his cooking skills while talking about his international travels and experiences in his characteristic humorous and charismatic manner.

Afterward, the lines outside Hilly's grew even longer, and Plĕas' menu had plenty that appealed to the young, hip crowd. Hilly was a popular man about town, who owned two restaurants and always attracted the in-crowd, who came and heard music, spoken word, and poetry. His inspired choice in a chef to make his restaurant not only fashionable, but also gastronomically appealing, was a solid move. Plĕas gave Hilly's the edge it needed, and he and Hilly remained friends for more than fifteen years.

Chapter 8
Growing Up Pearson

Lucille Pearson in her nurse uniform

Lucille was excelling in her new nursing career at Presbyterian Hospital. A naturally compassionate person, she was known for doing things like putting cards by the beds of patients who hadn't received visitors and took the time to get to know everyone in her care. Doctors and patients adored her, as she always put a smile on their faces when she came into the room.

The famous jazz musician, Lionel Hampton, was building two beautiful buildings on 131st Street, one name after his wife Glady's Hampton, and the other named Lionel Hampton Houses, after himself. I was very close with my mother, and never forgot the day we went to the rental office to get the application for the apartments being built by Lionel Hampton. It was such a special day for my mother when she applied. I watched her fill out the application. When we got home with such urgency; my mother had everything required to be eligible for this opportunity. This was all about her independence. "God doesn't come when you want, but he's always on time." My mother used to say this all the time. Well... she was right!

In 1973, my mother got the acceptance letter to move into her new apartment located at 273 West 131st Street. On move in day, it was my mother, and grandmother and myself. It was laid out as a penthouse apartment, with five bedrooms, one and a half bathrooms, a laundry on the top floor, and 24-hour security service. Because it was a brand-new building, it had the smell of fresh paint. Words could not have described the joy on my mother's face. She even attended the ribbon-cutting ceremony.

On her days off, my mother worked with a group of friends and neighbors in front of the Lionel Hampton Houses, and they walked around the communities, asking strangers to sign their names to the petition to make Martin Luther King Jr.'s birthday a legal holiday.

Even if her supervisor had her stay and do a double shift, she still walked down the streets to gather names, even if she had to go at it alone.

Lucille was committed to completing this necessary holiday mission. The fight to make Martin Luther King Jr's birthday a legal holiday took many people's campaigning and support, to spearhead this action.

People from all over wanted this necessary acknowledgment for King to happen, who—along with thousands of people across the country—petitioned to make Martin Luther King Jr.'s birthday a national holiday. The movement garnered the support of celebrities and politicians like Stevie Wonder, Edward "Ted" Kennedy, and even the National Football League (NFL).

My mother's efforts to establish a holiday for Martin Luther King's birthday came to fruition in 1983. On August 2nd, the House passed the resolution by a vote of 338 to 90, and Martin Luther King Day was established as a federal holiday in all fifty states. King was born on January 15th, 1929, in Atlanta, Georgia, but the holiday was to be celebrated on the third Monday of January.

My mother did live to celebrate the Martin Luther King Jr. holiday, however, she passed on the eve of the Martin Luther King Jr. Holiday in 1988. She passed away in her oldest son's arms, Plĕas Tusant Pearson III (Sonny), that night.

The funeral was held at the Mount Neboh Baptist Church in Harlem, where she was a member for more than twenty years and where her grandmother, Frances Coats, was eulogized five years earlier when she died peacefully at the age of ninety-three. The repast was held at the Lionel Hampton Houses Community Center. Both events were well-attended by her friends, family, and co-workers, who reminisced about the uniquely intelligent, motivated, and passionate woman who uplifted everyone she knew. From Lucille, her children learned to be passionate about the life they wanted to live and to make sure they left the world a better place than how they found it.

♥Lucille (Mommy)♥
I remember your red knit dress you wore with the gold chain belt and the long black gloves that went up to your elbows.
I remember the smell of your pocketbook, which consisted of Wrigley's (peppermint) chewing gum.
I used to smell the scent of your perfume on your handkerchief.
I remember your red lipstick on your favorite coffee cup.
I just wanted to reminisce for a quick second.
RIP, my Queen.
Jan

Sonny and Larry

Sonny and Larry, followed in their father's footsteps and entered the culinary arts. Plĕas taught them how to mix herbs and spices and added them *"until your ancestor taps you on the shoulder and tells you, that's enough."* He also taught them the business of culinary arts and hospitality, how to network and climb the ladder to success.

Sonny had a natural gift for wine expertise and developed a passion for understanding various domestic and international wines' tastes, techniques, and styles. Larry found his niche in the baking industry and agriculture profession. His natural intuition for combining ingredients allowed him to create innovative recipes for different loaves of bread and desserts, which earned him glowing reviews.

Both of them inherited the "Pearson charm" and their natural abilities, combined with their charismatic personalities, led them to establish strong connections with people from different countries. They both worked in different restaurants throughout their lives and met and established great relationships with other people, just like their father had done. As Plĕas said, food was the common denominator that brought people together from all over the world. Breaking bread together unified people.

Larry had three children Monica, Mary Frances, which she is the name's sake of Lucille's mother (Mary) and grandma (Frances), and George, the grandson who inherited his grandfather's name (Tusant). Sonny played a huge part in the family's children's lives, and he has so many godchildren whose lives he also contributed to, as well. Plĕas was blessed with plenty of family love.

Janell Pearson

Like the hustle in my grandmother Bessie, the soul of my father Plĕas, and the elegance of my mother Lucille (Mary and Frances), I, too, was determined to create my part in this world. Thinking like a natural-born leader, I was determined to become an entrepreneur.

I followed in my family's tradition of entrepreneurship and was a fast and proficient typist. I started earning money in college from typing up my classmates' term papers and resumes, and grew my clientele when I began advertising my services in local papers.

Soon, I started hiring employees and recruited women on public assistance and from unemployment offices that were in between work. Like my father, I offered job training and a means to support themselves, because I held typing and business skills classes right at my mother's dining room table. After a while, I expanded my business to include an answering service, temp agency, and messenger service. I advertised to lawyers, corporations, and from small to large business owners. I was so surprised how many calls I received for my services.

After college, I worked for a Fortune 500 company, and it was there, while I waited for a meeting to start in the conference room, that I realized I could mirror the services the company provided to be incorporated into my own community. Just like that, I knew my passion was not working at this company. I should be working for myself!

In September of 1981, at twenty-five years old, I became the President of my own corporation, T.M.A Enterprises, Inc., which provided typing/secretarial services, messenger, and office support. The business was located at 271 West 125th Street, between 7th and 8th Avenues. It catered to small and large businesses from an office services setup.

I noticed that some Black businesses could not afford an administrative staff to assist them and limited their success. My services allowed smaller businesses to take on larger corporate contracts. My office became their backup, and I assigned administrative assistants to work from my client's office or my business location as a temporary service.

I ran my business in a small office space, designed with just a reception area, a large copier, and a room with desks setup for support. I had a staff of fifteen, the support of my cousin Gail, LaShawn, my brother Sonny, and my cousin James as my first messenger, which others followed. My right-hand person, Debra, maintained my office.

My passion was to open a business in Harlem. My father was so happy for me! I followed in his footsteps and became an entrepreneur/business owner. What's more, Harlem came out to support my business.

I remembered when I told my father that T.M.A Enterprises, Inc. had picked up three more corporate accounts from midtown. He gave me a high five and said, "Go ahead, Ms. Pearson, you doing it!"

As my business grew, the demand for my services increased. I was able to stay in business for close to ten years. Besides having opened my business at a very young age, I also worked for some of the top companies in the United States. But, more importantly, like my father saw me, I became a woman of principle.

My dad was really impressed with my ongoing client list. As time went on, T.M.A Enterprises, Inc. gained clients like Freedom National Bank (a Black-owned bank), the world-renowned Boys' Choir of Harlem, the Apollo Theater, the Amsterdam News, Webber & Brooker Real Estate, and Tony Brown's Journal, just to mention a few.

Dr. Dorothy Irene Heights, President of the NCNW, patronized my business' secretarial services. My staff used to type her programs and format her documents. When Dorothy first visited-the office, it did not connect at first, that she was the "Honorable Dorothy Heights." She had a powerful presence, and even when we completed her projects, she stayed a little while longer and just smiled at me and my staff.

President Barack Obama called Dr. Dorothy Heights "the Godmother of the Civil Rights Movement." And, in 2017, she was honored on the United States postal stamp.

In 1986, I received an envelope announcing that President Dr. Dorothy Irene Heights had chosen me to receive the National Council of Negro Women (NCNW) award. I was honored along with singer Whitney Houston and Rev. Calvin O. Butts III of Abyssinian Baptist Church, and other honorees. I will never forget how proud my parents were of me. I knew my father was proud of me for accomplishing something on my own merit. To be acknowledged by Dorothy Height was like a dream come true.

Another award I received was in 1988. Dorothy Pitman Hughes hosted an awards dinner to acknowledge the leadership and business owners of Harlem. I was one of the honorees who received her award. What an honor it was to have received this award from another honorable and historic woman on that day and time!

After winning several other awards, I sold my business for a profit not long after giving birth to my daughter, Nikki, who had a big hand in caring for my father in his later years.

Chapter 9

He Lived His Life
to the Fullest

In 1984, Plĕas retired from the Sheraton Hotel and continued to cater privately. With his days free, he had more time to spend in Harlem and visited with his friends, children, and grandchildren. He was a proud grandfather.

Even though he lived fifty blocks south of his beloved Harlem, Plĕas came up to visit as often as he could, frequenting barbershops and the annual block party at St. Nick. He visited the campaign offices of his close friends Charles Rangel and David Dinkins both were known for their American political status—just to let them know they still had his support. If Plĕas was told of a neighbor that had passed, he made every effort to attend the service, out of respect. Even though he was not a multimillionaire, he made sure he left the family with some money in an envelope. He let their families know that they were appreciated.

When he wasn't traveling or visiting Harlem, Plĕas enjoyed taking walks in the community, or sitting on a bench in the park where he fed the pigeons. Locals all knew "the man with the beige trench coat and hat" who sat there regularly, and chatted with neighbors.

One day Plĕas took a long hard look at himself. He analyzed the people that loved him, those he loved, and some he hurt along the way—mainly because what was expected of him was different than his own expectations. Sometimes, he thought it was just the way he was raised. Plĕas felt he had to keep it moving; consistently learning life lessons was so important to him. When he could no longer make the half-mile walk, I found myself sitting in his place one afternoon and overheard people asking one another, "Hey, do you remember the older gentleman who used to sit here and feed the birds?" He read the Newspaper and use to give such good advice

I looked up at them and said, "Do you mean that man with the beige hat and the trench coat with the cane? That's my father!"

"Oh," they said. "We haven't seen him in a while."

One day, about five years before he passed, my father said to me, "Something ain't right. I'm starting to not remember things." Realizing what was happening, I started to record him telling his stories. Although those tapes were tragically destroyed, listening to him helped me further appreciate what a remarkable man he was and what an amazing life he led. More important, he showed me that you can have varying chapters in this one life.

Eventually, my father was diagnosed with Sundown Syndrome, a form of Alzheimer's that affected patients mainly in the late afternoons and evenings. Sufferers are often kept up at night by strong memories of the past, and, during these episodes, my father called me and recounted stories from his life that came to mind. Nikki, who had just graduated college and entering her new opportunities, dedicated herself to managing his care: created his schedule, kept track of the nurse attendants who watched over him, and left reminder notes around the apartment.

Regularly interested in current events, Plĕas was glued to the television news when Obama ran for president. The election filled him with energy and excitement.

He said, "It's like the lottery. You gotta keep watching what the numbers are doing."

During the election, my father stayed up for three nights, watching the results and called me with updates. Then, on the night of the actual election, he called me and said, "Did you know Barack has the same birthday as Lucille on August 4th?" Later, we realized she died on Michelle Obama's birthday, January 17th.

Hearing him filled with so much life and excitement reminded me of the strong man he was.

The election invigorated him, and he was like his old self for a short time. When the results finally came in on November 4th, they announced that Obama had won, and became the 44th President of the United States, he wept with joy.

When I visited the next day, he cried again and, as tears streamed down his cheeks, he said, "Baby, do you know how many people didn't live to see this moment? They were there fighting, but they didn't get to see it. But I'll tell them when I get there."

Then he said, "Don't you ever forget that prayer changes things."

On August 18th, 2011, Plĕas passed, peacefully in his sleep at eighty-nine. I recalled receiving the call about my father's passing and rushed to his apartment. Once there, I noticed a uniformed police officer and my husband who stood on either side of his bed. Somehow, my attention averted to the window left open by his nursing attendant, and a wave of comfort passed over me as I knew that, through it, my father's spirit had been set free, and joined his ancestors in the next life.

My father always had a zeal for life and was never afraid to fight for what was right because he knew

God was with him. He was a protector to his family, a charismatic leader to the outside world, and a possibility thinker. To know him was to love him. On his tombstone, it is written: "He lived his life to the fullest."

Afterword

While everyone has their special community, they
call home the neighborhood that represents
them, almost as if it's a reflection of their soul. Well, in
the case of Mr. Plĕas Tusant Pearson, that special place
was Harlem. Plĕas recognized Harlem's power and in-
trinsic talent and gifts the day he visited while he worked on the Seabo Railroad. He wanted to be a part of
it and contributed to its purpose. Even though he was
from Birmingham, Alabama, it always held a special
place in his heart. Harlem lit a flame in his heart that
burned for the rest of his life.

Every action Plĕas did was never for fame or attention. He believed in his community and wanted to do
his part to help nurture it.

Gentrification

My father foresaw the gentrification of Harlem and
was not surprised, but he wondered how many Black
people were employed to help build those beautiful high-rise apartments? Today, longtime residents

are being forced out of their own neighborhood by dramatic rent increases.

What do you do when the displacement becomes all too real? Efforts need to be made to prevent the continued "milking down" of 125th Street from unique, Black-owned businesses to big expensive retail stores that Black people can't afford to shop in. Today, local mom and pop businesses are replaced by coffee shops. Costly luxury condos went up left and right. The new clothing stores don't represent the culture and style of the community. The community atmosphere should never be lost, like walking to our neighborhood soul food restaurants, or going to our local bodega stores and being greeted by Mr. Garcia while he listened to his Salsa music.

As my father said, Black representatives needed to be at every board meeting, looking over the development, construction and overall infrastructure plans coming to Harlem. Our neighborhood, with its beautiful architecture and unparalleled commutability to other parts of the city and the tri-state area, has appealed to gentrifiers who would never be able to afford such a beautiful home in another part of the city.

Dad used to say, "Don't get me wrong. I want the development of Harlem to happen. But never forget that Black people were refused bank loans to develop their own neighborhood." Those same loans were granted to white people. It must be remembered that Harlem could and should have been as powerful as Black Wall Street, if only we were given access to that capital.

In another twenty years, we could feel like we are the visitors instead of the ones who were born and raised in Harlem. But even if we do have to move out of Harlem, we must find a way to give back, and maintain the institutions and people who remain.

Fifty years ago, Dad felt the reason he fought so hard for Harlem, especially when he shut down some of the construction sites to hire our men and women in our communities, was because he understood that ultimately the city knew Harlem would be home to white people, too.

Today, real estate agencies desiring to appeal to these urban pioneers are calling the neighborhood SoHa, for "South Harlem." But Harlem stood up and fought that action, thank you to the community activist and leaders, I have no doubt that if my father was here today he would have been by your side.

What my father predicted is coming to pass. He knew the key to the favorable development of Harlem's future was to have formed a united and powerful community collaboration so we could all be a part of the new growth.

After all that we have been through as a race, Black people have maintained our essence, from

Africa to the Harlem Renaissance, through the '50s, '60s, and up until today. We never let white people break our spirit and our entrepreneurial status here in America, and we need to remain vigilant and true to that conviction.

My father always said it was okay for other cultures to come and join the community. Still, they should do so with a spirit of maintaining the culture that attracted them to the neighborhood in the first place, while also contributing their own cultural flavor. The rich legacy of Harlem can be enjoyed by everyone, as can the benefits of the influx of other cultures, their restaurants, stores, and businesses.

As I write this, I think of all the people whose lives my father touched. Many of them have reached out, letting me know they are being priced out of Harlem and relocated to other places.

Change, of course, is the only constant, and some of these changes have been positive, but the challenge is for Harlem's distinctive culture and history for future generations to be retained.

When my dad thought of Harlem, he thought of home: the food, the culture, and the style. To him, Harlem had its own language, and it was his heaven on earth. As Dad got older, this passion for Harlem never died.

He did everything he could within his frame of capabilities and never let his limitations put a hold on him or what he tried to accomplish. He saw opportunity where most did not. Every action Plĕas did, was never for fame or attention; he believed in his community and wanted to do his part to nurture it.

One morning in 2010, while having breakfast with my father in Harlem, he said he wanted to see some of the new high-rise apartment buildings going up and asked me to take him for a drive around the neighborhood. It was early in the morning, around 6 AM., when we started on the west side, and the first thing we saw was a white couple walking their pit bull.

My father laughed so hard. "So, this is the new face of Harlem?" He shook his head. "Well," he said, "that's fine."

Unsung Heroes

Unsung heroes, we see them throughout our daily routine, working within our healthcare system, our educators. We waited for them to check us out at our local grocery stores. We saw them pass out food to the homeless on the streets. We saw them call out an injustice and fight to make things right. Overall, we saw them making our daily lives better, in the simplest and overlooked (and, at times, the most unrewarded) ways. Why? This question can be answered in so many ways. However, that is not the point! What is important is that we use or follow their unaverred and selfless actions for years to come.

Man in The Middle

The Strength of Harlem is a book based on the life and times of Mr. Plĕas Tusant Pearson and his passion for being an advocate and entrepreneur, while he followed his God-given talent, fought to end the discrimination against Black construction workers in Harlem, job training, providing private car service and became one of the first Black Chef as a guest on a major network TV show. He loved his community and his people. Muhammad Ali and Malcolm X saw that and respected it. In addition, his willingness to do what he could within his reach to enhance the Black culture was commendable.

Please make no mistake. He was an "unsung hero" not because he was seen in a photo with these two great men, but because of his enduring actions to stand up for Black people during the most challenging times in America. He believed in Black liberation and equality for all. He wanted his people to thrive so future generations could be successful. He knew he could only do so much. However, he was willing to do what he could regarding the circumstances, and for that, his story had to be told.

As you can see, he was much more than a man in the middle!

There are many unsung heroes in this world like, Mr. Plĕas Tusant Pearson. Sadly, they do not get recognized for their loyalty and selfless acts; yet, they should be recognized for all they have accomplished. That's why it's important for young people to talk to their grandparents, fathers, mothers, and other family members if they are blessed to still have them in their lives. When you have your own children, you can begin to build your own legacy.

The Strength Point Publishing Boutique is based on helping people tell their stories. The boutique finds a way to reveal untold deeds from a person's life and create a hearty and visual way to tell their story, modeling content relatable to everyday people.

That is why I named my publishing company "Strength Point Publishing."

Let us tell your unsung story. I promise it will be worth it!

Additionally, I knew it would encourage others to tell their unsung stories.

For my readers, I want to thank you so much for taking the time to read this book. I truly hope you have taken something positive and encouraging from it.

Contact Information:

Publishing Company, Strength Point Publishing, Inc.
Website: www.strengthpointpublishing.com
Email:info@strengthpointpublishing.com
Website:www.forthestrengthofharlem.com
Email: info@forthestrengthofharlem.com
Phone Number: (347) 281-1742

Funny Memories
Sayings by Plĕas Tusant Pearson

On some Saturdays, my friends and I practiced our dance moves in the living room as we watched Soul Train. One of my funniest memories with my dad was when he put on a James Brown record, thinking he was going to show off his dance moves during one of those days.

Then, he started doing the Boogaloo, taking three steps to the left and then three steps to the right with his fist and thumb pointing out like he was trying to get a lift somewhere.

Oh… he thought he was so smooth. It was so funny. My friends and I used to laugh so hard at him. We just got on the floor and started doing the Boogaloo dance, too! … GOOD TIMES.

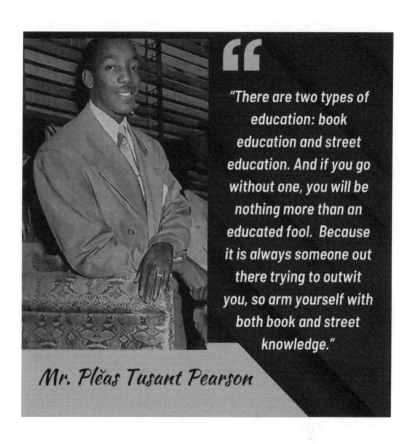

"There are two types of education: book education and street education. And if you go without one, you will be nothing more than an educated fool. Because it is always someone out there trying to outwit you, so arm yourself with both book and street knowledge."

Mr. Plĕas Tusant Pearson

EVEN A MILLIONAIRE
MUST STAY ON HIS
GRIND
BECAUSE IF HE
SPENDS $1, HE'S NO
LONGER
A MILLIONAIRE

Plēs Tusant Pearson

PHOTO COLLAGE

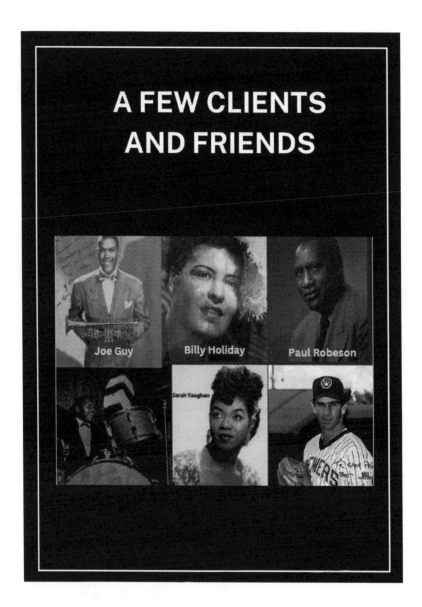

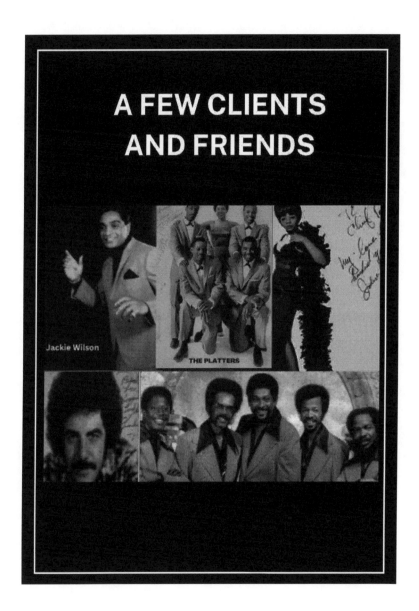

Acknowledgements

WOW! I have finally completed my father's biographical memoir, and this journey unearthed so many emotions. I knew it was my destiny to complete this book for my family and future generations to come, as well as share his story with the people of Harlem and the historians and people who love to read about unsung heroes. By sharing Plĕas Tusant Pearson's story, that was only previously shared through family conversations, it has now become our family's history and legacy. I'm sure there are other unsung heroes whose stories are just waiting to be told as well.

As I reflect on the people who encouraged me to proceed on this path, I just wanted to take this time to show my gratitude for their support.

I could not complete this book without thanking people that made a difference in my life. These names are in no particular order.

Thomas, my **husband,** thank you for the fantastic graphic design book cover and website. I appreciate your continuous support in every new project I have taken on.

Sherrell (aka Nikki), my daughter, my mini-me, I'm so proud of you. Anyone that knows me has heard me say, on more than one occasion, that I gave birth to my best friend. Thank you so much for all the days and nights you contributed to the family stories, and some of the stories I even forgot. Your grandpa would have been proud of you. I'm excited about what the future holds for you. Just remember, God will do amazing things in your life. Keep moving forward, my child. Love, Mommy!

Sonny (Plĕas), my big brother, your contribution to dad's story and providing some of the photos were pinnacle to the book. You have always been there for me in my most critical and most vulnerable times in my life. Even when we disagreed on certain things, it never got in the way of us having each other's back. Those moments taught me more than you will ever know.

Larry, my brother, you have a world of knowledge because you enjoy reading all subject matters to enrich your thinking. You remember what Dad and

Mom instilled in us, which was the art of cooking with whatever you had in your cabinet. One more thing, I recently looked at you and Cheryl's beautiful wedding photo, and I remember how happy Dad was on that day.

Gail, Curtis Sr., and Curtis Jr. Gail, I still cherish the sweet memories we had. You saw my first customer walk in the door on 125th Street. And I still remember all our trips to Alabama with the kids.

Curtis Sr., your music has always touched the hearts of many, especially at the right time and moment. Music is genuinely your God-given gift (along with your sense of humor). **Curtis Jr.,** love you to pieces.

James, my cousin, I don't want you to think for one moment I forgot the support you gave me when I needed you. Thank you. When I was a single mother, you told me to keep a bat beside my door, for protection. I still keep a bat close by, even today. LOL!

George and Mary Frances, I'm so happy you wanted to know more about our family history. Your questions helped me understand how important it was to complete this book for the next generation. Love you guys!

Monica, Tyeonna, and Gabrielle, continue to support each other. He kept you all in his prayers.

Kim and Stacy, continue to grow the beautiful bond you have with each other as sisters. Remember the love Uncle Plĕas had for you two.

Detroit Family, your granddad truly loved each and every one of you. He used to talk about his Detroit family with a smile on his face. I wish he were here to see the close-knit family we have become. Much love!

LaShawn and **Debra,** it's been years since we have spoken; however, I would like to take this time to acknowledge your hard work and for helping me support my customers at T.M.A Enterprises Inc. For that, I thank you!

Dindga McCannon, you have been a friend to the Pearson family for more than forty years. We have admired your impressive talents as an artist—your murals, illustration, fiber art, and so much more—which are respected around the world. Thank you for being in my life.

Louise, for more than forty years, you have never missed sending me a birthday card, and you know I'm older than that today. LOL! That's one thing my dad knew he would get in the mail as well. You are the heart of friendship, and I adore you.

A very special thanks to **Lisa- Mr. Byrd's** daughter and her team, for continuing her father's legacy – to all the **Old Timers** and the **new St. Nick family**, much love. Especially to **Mr. Byrd** (RIP), you gave me my first summer job. After asking me what I wanted to do with my life, I quickly replied and said, "I want to become a businesswoman." And, for four summers through the Summer Youth Program, the opportunity that I didn't know was an opportunity at the time, you put me in the rent office to help the ladies. That experience changed my world and future. Thank you!

J. Barrett (Dad's godson) and **Shirley** who kept in contact with the family during the hard times and still today. Thank you!

Old Co-Workers, thank you guys for your support. Most of you enjoy reading books on your weekends. Well, this will be a short read, but a good one. Thank you!

To those that have passed on, my special angels thank you for your unconditional love. Each one of you made a difference in my life, your spirit will live within me always: my mother, grandmothers Frances, Mary, Aunt Mildred, Lula and Aunt Jackie.

Uncle Carter (RIP). You were our family's rock, our tall giant. You took on a lot for our family. I can't imagine where the family would have been without your love and support. THANK YOU!

Pat, my cousin, thank you for being there for me when I was a young teenager with so many questions. To this day, I appreciate your knowledge.

Penny, I still use your delicious oxtail recipe. LOL! Dad and I used to talk about how contagious your laughter was, and it makes me smile when I think about it today

Debra, my cousin, I'm glad you returned to my life. You came back with your unbelievable memories and details about our childhood. I really enjoyed our weekly talks and your encouragement. Thank you for all your support! RIP.

Go-Go (RIP, Derrell), thank you for getting me out of my office and making sure I showed up to the best parties and clubs that were hot back in the day, like the Shadow, Leviticus, and Bentleys. After-work parties—ladies got in free before 7:00 p.m. LOL! You were truly a good friend. Miss you!

To my father's friends and prayer warriors at Mount Sinai Cathedral Church of God in Christ. **Ms. Hattie** (RIP), and church members. Thank you!

Along with a host of family, friends,
and associates,
THANK YOU FROM THE
BOTTOM OF MY HEART!

Picture Credits

Please note, the historical timeline on Plĕas Tusant Pearson story was based on his personal collection of photos which he appears in for supporting material.

Other pictures are credited and acknowledge as resources. Howard L. Bingham, Wikimedia Commons.

About the Author

JANELL PEARSON, first time Author, was born and raised in Harlem, New York City. She became an entrepreneur at the early age of 25. In 1981, she opened her first business, named T.M.A. Enterprises, Inc. on 125th Street, which provided secretarial services, messenger, and office business support. She appeared in articles from the Amsterdam News and other significant media newspapers, to be acknowledged for being so young as a successful businesswoman. She wears her positive thinking as her "Superpower."

The entrepreneur & author is an esteemed multi-award winner and recognized for her work by the NCNW (National Council of Negro Women). 1986, she received an award from the Honorable Dorothy Heights of the National Council of Negro Women (NCNW). In 1988, Janell received an award from Dorothy Pittman Hughes, another Honorable Black historical leader. After ten years, Janell returned to work in the corporate sector, where she thrived in mostly fortune 500 companies for 30 years.

Janell is an active member of the Harlem Writers Guild. One of the world's oldest continuously operated African American Writers Guild in the world.